Presenting with
Power

Practical books that inspire

Communicating Across Cultures
How to break down international barriers to business communications

The Ten Career Commandments
Equip yourself with the 10 most important skills to move up the career ladder

CVs for High Flyers
Move up the career ladder with a CV that gets you noticed

Making Workshops Work
Ensure your workshops create high-octane interaction

Communicate with Emotional Intelligence
Use personal competencies and key relationship skills to influence others and get results

Send for a free copy of the latest catalogue to:

How To Books
3 Newtec Place, Magdalen Road,
Oxford OX4 1RE, United Kingdom
email: info@howtobooks.co.uk
http://www.howtobooks.co.uk

Presenting
with
Power

Captivate, Motivate,
Inspire and Persuade

SHAY McCONNON

howtobooks

Published in 2002 by
How To Books Ltd,
3 Newtec Place,
Magdalen Road,
Oxford, OX4 1RE, United Kingdom.
Tel: (01865) 793806.   Fax: (01865) 248780.
email: info@howtobooks.co.uk
http://www.howtobooks.co.uk

British Library Cataloguing in Publication Data
A catalogue record for this book is available from
the British Library.

Edited by David Kershaw
Cover design by Baseline Arts Ltd, Oxford

Produced for How To Books by Deer Park Productions
Typeset by Anneset, Weston-super-Mare, North Somerset
Printed and bound by Cromwell Press, Trowbridge, Wiltshire

Note: The material contained in this book is set out in good
faith for general guidance and no liability can be accepted
for loss or expense incurred as a result of relying in particular
circumstances on statements made in the book. The laws and
regulations are complex and liable to change, and readers should
check the current position with the relevant authorities before
making personal arrangements.

Be sincere, be brief, be seated

(Franklin D. Roosevelt)

Contents

Here is a collection of 'ad-libs' that might be useful for overcoming those 'awful' moments.

Preface

Your ability to communicate is the single most important factor in your professional tool bag. People who make a difference, who inspire others, who get promoted are usually excellent communicators. They are able to present ideas clearly and convincingly, they are able to lead and excite, they motivate and persuade. Excellence in management is impossible without excellence in communication. The people who have shaped the course of history were all excellent communicators. They could move audiences, win minds and hearts and get people to take action.

The need to communicate is even greater in today's fast-changing workplace where hierarchies are being dismantled and information sharing is becoming the task of the many and no longer the domain of the executives. Of all the ways you communicate (by letter, e-mail, telephone or one-to-one conversations). the one that gives you the greatest chance to make a powerful impact is the presentation.

MOST GREAT SPEAKERS WERE ONCE POOR SPEAKERS

John was a bright, warm, fun type of person. But this was not how he came across when he made a presentation. He was dry, serious, stiff and very nervous. What was going on? Where was his warmth? What happened to his likeable personality? It was as if when he stood up to speak his real personality could not show through. Instead, he became frightened, self-conscious and feared his mind would go blank. John is not unusual. In a recent survey of phobias, public speaking ranked second to rats but beat death into third place on the dread list. It appears that many people would prefer to die than make a presentation! Many of today's great speakers were once poor speakers and they too suffered from anxiety and lacked confidence. They became great speakers by finding opportunities to speak, uncomfortable as it was for them. That's how we become good at anything – by doing the uncomfortable with skilful guidance. To excel at driving, you need a car and a driving instructor. You, the reader, need to find the opportunities to present. This book can be your guide and coach, your speaking instructor, if you like.

This is no ordinary book on presentations. While it covers all you need to know about researching your material, structuring your message and designing your visual aids, it also shows you ways to develop confidence and gives tips on how to deliver. Few books deal with the psychology of communicating. This book will introduce you to personality types, and you will learn why some people will want you to be short and snappy, why others will want to 'connect' with you and why others will want precise, accurate information.

In this book I share with you the secrets that professional speakers use to impact dramatically on the audience and to make a memorable impression. I also include a section on how to appear quick-witted, spontaneous and professional when the unexpected happens (such as fire alarms going off or you drop something).

Whether you are a novice speaker or a seasoned pro, this book will give you tips and techniques that will take you to the next level.

You will learn how to:

◆ captivate
◆ motivate
◆ inspire
◆ persuade
◆ and much more.

This is a practical, no nonsense, easy-to-read book that is full of help and advice for people who want to enjoy presenting powerfully.

Shay McConnon

1

Planning Your Presentation

In this chapter:

◆ preparing in stages
◆ setting your objectives
◆ creating a take-home message
◆ researching your audience
◆ generating ideas
◆ planning your presentation mind map.

The deadline approaches and you finally sit down to prepare your talk, unable to find any more excuses for putting it off. You search for inspiration and desperately seek an opening line.

You struggle. Nothing seems appropriate. You try three or four openings and they all end up in the waste-paper bin.

Eventually inspiration comes and you begin writing. 'Good morning, everyone. When Terry asked me to present I thought . . . ' and off you go. Is this a good way to start? Probably not. You are running with what comes off the top of your head. This is likely to be haphazard, lack structure and may not be related to your audience's needs.

The place to start preparing a presentation is not your opening – although that is the start when you finally deliver. You need to start with why you are delivering and what you want to achieve.

What is required is a route or map that shows where you want to go and how you want to get there, and of course you must know why you want to go there.

Before you start ask yourself these questions:

- ◆ Why am I speaking?
- ◆ Whom am I speaking to?
- ◆ What do they need from me?
- ◆ What do I say?
- ◆ How do I construct my message?
- ◆ How do I deliver it?

PREPARATION IS KEY

The casual, seemingly effortless presentation is likely to be the result of a great deal of planning, research and hard work. If you fail to prepare, you are preparing to fail. In the same way as you build a house in stages, so you can develop your presentation in a structured, layered way.

The planning and research phase is like laying the foundation. Although never seen, the final product stands, cracks or falls because of it. On this foundation you lay the bricks for your presentation by generating ideas and structuring what you are going to say. The rooms can be your key ideas. And, of course, you need to decorate the rooms – the visual aids, anecdotes and supporting evidence.

You might pay particular attention to the front view people get of your house . . . how you open your presentation. And finally add those finishing touches, which come from your unique personality and style.

PREPARING IN STAGES

Don't expect to sit down and write your presentation in one sitting. Before you write your presentation, you will need to clarify your objectives, understand your audience and research your topic. Only then will you be in a position to structure your message, decide on your key points, put an opening and a closing together and add supplementary material for impact. After that you need to prepare yourself as the speaker, practise delivery and get yourself into a confident state to present.

SETTING YOUR OBJECTIVES

It will be easier for you to decide what to say in your presentation if you know:

◆ your primary objectives;
◆ your secondary objectives;
◆ your take–home message; and
◆ something about your audience.

Your primary objective

The most fundamental thing in preparing your presentation is to have a clear objective. Unless you know where you are going, how can you begin the journey? It is essential that you are clear about what you want to achieve. What is your goal? Why are you presenting? If your objective is unclear, you are likely to end up where you don't want to be. Like any good navigator, once you are clear about your destination, you can more easily identify the route to that powerful presentation.

In clarifying your primary objective, think in terms of your listeners and how you want to impact on them. After your audience have listened to you, how do you want them to:

◆ think
◆ feel
◆ do?

The more <u>specific</u> you are with your answers, the more helpful your objectives are likely to be.

These are not objectives:

◆ 'I'm speaking because it's the annual sales conference'
◆ 'I'm speaking because I am the regional sales manager'

You may wish to think ahead to your next presentation by writing your objectives in the box below.

What I want my audience:
To think _____
_____
To feel _____
_____
To do _____
_____

Your secondary objectives

Your primary objective might be to get the Board to agree next year's sales figures. However other things may also be important to you. For example, you may wish to project a highly professional image of the sales team.

Here are some examples of secondary objectives:

- inform
- entertain
- persuade
- explore
- sell
- get support
- influence behaviour
- communicate an image
- provoke feelings
- motivate
- stimulate new ideas and approaches
- reassure
- challenge
- arouse curiosity.

You may wish to think ahead to your next presentation by writing your secondary objectives in the box below.

My secondary objectives:

1 _____

_____

2 _____

_____

Creating your take-home message

If you had only 30 seconds to speak, what is the one thing you would want your audience to hear from you? Your take-home message is like a slogan for your talk. It needs to be catchy, easy to remember, compelling and thought provoking. It is the essence of your talk in a phrase or sentence.

You may wish to think ahead to your next presentation by writing your take-home message in the following box.

My take-home message is:

_____

_____

_____

_____

_____

Suggestion

Write your primary and secondary objectives and take-home message on Day Glo stars you can buy in stationery shops. Post these in a prominent place as you prepare your presentation. These 'stars' can then help you decide on what to say and how best to say it without losing sight of your overall aim.

RESEARCHING YOUR AUDIENCE

After identifying your objective (what it is you want to achieve), the next step is to consider your audience. It is vital to your preparation that you put yourself in the shoes of your audience, thinking about why they are coming, what they hope to gain, their feelings, concerns, issues and needs.

A presentation that doesn't connect with your audience's world will never be a good presentation. You will need to know if they are hands-on people, managers or customers:

◆ What experience do they have?
◆ How well do they know you?
◆ How do they feel about you?
◆ Do they know your responsibilities and areas of expertise?
◆ Are they likely to be resistant or apathetic?
◆ What do they need from you?

Answering these and similar questions will enable you to build a profile of your audience so you can pitch your presentation at the appropriate level. Figure 1 suggests a structure that might help you to create a profile of your audience – an audience portrait, if you like.

Think ahead to your next presentation and ask:

◆ Why should this audience listen to me?
◆ How will they benefit from what I have to say?

The answers to these questions will be useful in creating an attention-getting opening for your presentation.

The following questions will flush out useful information to help you with planning your presentation:

◆ Who is organising the event?
◆ What is the size and shape of the room?
◆ What equipment will be available?
◆ Who is speaking before you?
◆ Who will be introducing you?

Number of people attending:

_____

_____

Roles and responsibilities:

_____

_____

Experience and background:

_____

_____

Knowledge of subject being presented:

_____

_____

Attitude to me as presenter:

_____

_____

What do they need from me?

_____

_____

Key players in the audience:

_____

_____

Problem areas:

_____

_____

Likely objections:

_____

_____

Other considerations:

• Interests _____

• Sympathies _____

• Gender _____

• Age _____

• Education _____

Fig. 1.   An audience profile.

GENERATING IDEAS

Now you know what you want to achieve and what your audience needs, you are in a position to generate ideas and then begin writing. Many of your best ideas are likely to come at inconvenient moments: 3 o' clock in the morning; driving on the motorway, or having a bath. There are many ways of generating ideas, but stick with what works for you. If you suffer the blank mind syndrome, you may wish to pin a large sheet of plain paper to the wall weeks before your presentation and record ideas as you think of them.

Tony Buzan suggests that the brain does not always work in a linear format – it also acts on triggers that stimulate new thoughts. He has created mind maps, which facilitate thinking in both lateral and horizontal ways.

To create a mind map, draw a box in the centre of a blank page and note your presentation title in this box. Now jot down your main ideas on lines that radiate from the centre box. As each idea triggers others, jot those down as sub-branches of the main idea. Leave plenty of space for new thoughts. To keep the creativity flowing, jot down everything – even those weird, impractical ideas.

The aim here is to free up the mind to generate as many ideas as possible. Creativity will be restricted if you assess whether the ideas are useful. Evaluation comes later when you begin constructing your message. Just put down everything on paper and keep those creative juices flowing.

Suggestion
- ◆ No evaluation or criticism during this stage.
- ◆ Go for quantity not quality.
- ◆ Note all your ideas – even those way-out ones.

Tips for getting unstuck

If you get stuck for ideas, why not imagine different people presenting this talk (the prime minister, the MD, your mother, Mickey Mouse), and just imagine what they would say and how they would go about it.

Some other things you may want to try are as follows:

- ◆ Put yourself in the audience's shoes.
- ◆ Talk to other people about your topic and get their ideas.
- ◆ Get away from it all – take some exercise.
- ◆ Break your routine.
- ◆ Keep a pad and pen by your bed for those middle-of-the-night ideas.

Doing research

A good starting point for research is to review some of the leading books on your topic. Sources of information include newspaper and magazine articles, trade journals, colleagues and, of course, the Internet. Exploring such sources takes time.

The Internet brings an international electronic library right to your desk. The more specific your key words, the better-quality sites you are likely to access. Use well chosen key words to search for relevant reference material.

Planning your presentation mind map

Figure 2 is an example of a mind map devoted to planning a presentation. You may wish to use this to guide you in preparing future presentations.

SUMMARY

◆ Preparation is vital to a successful presentation.
◆ Begin with your objectives, not the opening to your presentation.
◆ Make your objectives specific.
◆ Create a catchy take-home message.
◆ Identify the needs of your audience.
◆ Brainstorm for ideas.

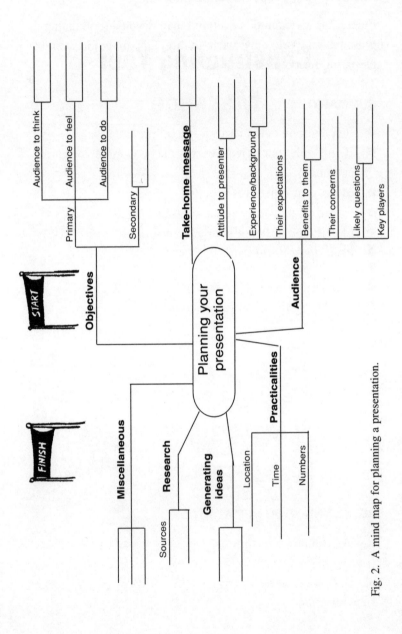

Fig. 2. A mind map for planning a presentation.

$\left(\ 2\ \right)$

Constructing Your
Message

In this chapter:

◆   selecting your key points
◆   creating a template for constructing your message
◆   writing your presentation
◆   condensing your script to notes
◆   tips for writing your presentation.

SELECTING YOUR KEY POINTS

Having completed your mind map over days or even weeks, you are likely to have a mass of ideas, some of which will support your objectives, others will not. How do you make your selection?

The Day Glo stars on which you have written your objectives will guide you in this selection. What ideas are best suited for achieving your objectives and meeting the needs of your audience? You may wish to prioritise the ideas you have generated by awarding them ticks. Three ticks if the idea is very important to your objectives. Two ticks if it is important and one tick for an unimportant idea. *If it doesn't support your objectives, don't include it.*

THREE KEY IDEAS

Beware of overloading your audience by giving them too much information. The human mind is limited in what it can retain and process. It is suggested that every great presentation contains at least one, but not more than three, key ideas. It is also suggested to have three supporting points for each key idea – anecdotes, metaphors or hard evidence that support your key idea. Always keep in mind what your audience need from you as you construct your message.

CREATING A TEMPLATE FOR CONSTRUCTING YOUR MESSAGE

The following is a logical and simple structure that provides continuity between the beginning, middle and end of your presentation. It is a framework that will help you construct a balanced presentation.

Opening

The opening is less about opening your presentation and more about opening up your audience so they will be receptive to you and your message. It's a bit like offering a handshake to your audience.

To develop an original and captivating opening requires careful planning. It is best left until you have decided on the main body of your presentation. Chapter 4 shows you how to open with impact.

Overview

The overview provides a brief outline of your talk. It gives the audience an insight into the theme and structure of your presentation. This not only lets the audience know what to expect, but enhances your credibility as a speaker who is organised and thorough. By talking benefits to audience rather than content, you will generate a higher level of interest.

Key idea 1

Begin with a general picture – the long shot, if you like. This is really a big picture statement of your first key idea. Now substantiate this with evidence. Create your argument in digestible bits for your audience. Break your key idea into segments. Finally, provide the close-up shot with examples, metaphors, quotations, statistical data, props, visual aids, anecdotes and critical commentary.

Transitions

Transitions are best if they are seamless. You are moving from one point to another without people being aware of the join. A useful way to do this is to recap on the previous segment and create a reason for moving to the next main point.

Key ideas 2 and 3

Repeat this process for the other main ideas.

Recap

Having presented your main points, you can now wrap up by bringing together the key elements of your presentation. You tell them what you have told them, but in a different way. For example:

So to summarise, the successful presenter – like a good trial lawyer – would get the jury's attention, then build his or her case and end with a plea to the judge and jury.

Closing

Make your ending brief, catchy and memorable. This is the time to use your take-home message and leave the audience feeling good and ready for action. Again, because of the importance of this, it is given specialist treatment in Chapter 4.

You may wish to use the structure shown in Figure 3 when constructing your next presentation.

WRITING YOUR PRESENTATION

Should you write it?

If you are inexperienced you may wish to begin by writing a full draft of your presentation, including anecdotes, metaphors and anything you intend to use. This ensures you are totally familiar with your topic and with what exactly you are going to say.

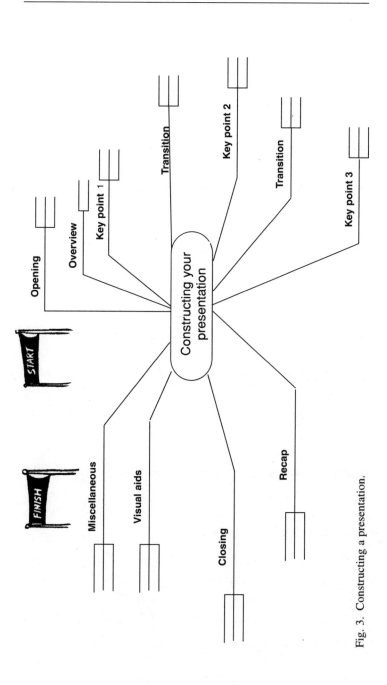

Fig. 3. Constructing a presentation.

Beware, however – the written word is designed to be read, not spoken. Written language is likely to be more formal and stilted. The language of writing is different from the language of speaking. Read aloud an article from the newspaper and you will understand this. Remember, you are a presenter not a speechwriter.

It will help to keep your sentence construction simple. Imagine you are talking to a friend and then write what you find yourself saying. If you are not sure if you sound natural, tape record a section of what you have written and amend where necessary.

Beware of putting too much talk into your talk

Make it easy for people to remember your key points. Less is better. Seldom do you hear people complain about a presentation being too short. Cut out the unnecessary points and words.   Leave them wanting more, rather than giving them everything you know about the topic. Rather than telling them everything you know, tell them everything they need to know. You might want to adopt the following as a guiding principle: stand up, speak up and shut up. Less is likely to be better.

Condensing your script to notes

Speaking from notes has all the benefits of impromptu speaking and none of the drawbacks of reading. Your safety net is a set of notes indicating key points. Transfer key ideas, phrases and prompts on to cards and simply glance at your notes from time to time to check your next point.

Index cards 102 mm by 152 mm are suitable for this. They are easy to manage and are less distracting than sheets of A4 paper. You can hold them in your hand or rest them on the lectern or table. Should you suffer from trembling hands, cards won't reveal this as much as a flapping piece of paper. Some speakers tie a treasury tag through a punched hole to keep the cards together. If not, be sure to number them as dropping unnumbered cards can be a calamity.

Making notes

Ideally, notes should be:

◆ easily visible – use different font sizes, colours, underline, capitals, etc.;
◆ minimal – only put down what you have to, otherwise there is the danger you will write the speech;
◆ abbreviated; and
◆ in pictures as well as in words.

Using notes

When using your notes, bear in mind the following points:

◆ Don't apologise for making reference to your notes. Notes can aid your credibility.
◆ Rather than steal a glimpse, look at them. Having notes tells your audience you are planned.
◆ Beware of talking into your notes. Pause and look at your notes and then speak to your audience.
◆ Open and close your presentation looking at your audience, not at your notes.
◆ Beware of shuffling or playing with your notes.

Should you memorise your speech?

It is difficult to communicate with your audience if you are struggling to remember each word of your speech. There is the real danger that your talk will sound mechanical and will lack spontaneity. Memorising can create the fear of forgetting. When you forget your lines, there are no retakes, no stopping of the action. The show must go on.

Using storyboards

Some presenters use the storyboard format for their notes. The makers of films and TV programmes use storyboards. Sketch your ideas on paper: just add stick figures, faces, symbols, key words – anything that will have meaning for you and triggers a picture in your mind. You are likely to find it easier to remember your presentation from picture notes and you are likely to create pictures in the minds of your audience, making you 'easy' to listen to.

Tips for writing your presentation

Just write what comes into your head – it may be your opening, closing or a point that is useful to make. Get it down on paper. Don't judge it at this stage and don't think too hard or too long – just get the ideas and words flowing. Trust your creative side.

Write as quickly as you can and stop when your ideas are out. Repeat this at another time. You might want to do this for five minutes a day for a week Sometimes you have to write for a while before you find out what it is you want to say. Writing can be an excellent way of clarifying your ideas.

Use this 'quick write' as the basis for your written presentation, redrafting it as often as you need to reach the standard you want. The important thing is not to try to get it right first time – that comes with the drafting.

Read through your draft to ensure you have included all the key points. Now add anecdotes, humour and topicality if these are important to you.

Summary

◆ Select your key ideas with your objectives in mind.

◆ Follow a structure for constructing a balanced presentation.

◆ Writing can clarify your ideas.

◆ Beware of memorising or reading your script.

◆ Use notes so you come across as natural, spontaneous and fresh.

◆ Storyboard notes can be easier to remember.

3

Choosing your Visual Aids

In this chapter:

◆ making your messages visual
◆ designing visuals
◆ techniques for using visual aids
◆ using computer-based displays.

With advancements in technology, many people have become enamoured of multimedia and computer-generated slide presentations. While high-tech tools for visual aids have their place, they are not always the best choice for all presentations.

Choose what is best for the situation and never forget that *you* are the most powerful of all your visual aids: your dress, posture and facial expression.

MAKING YOUR MESSAGES VISUAL

In today's visual society of TV, computers and films, visuals are essential if you wish to make an impact. Mohamed Ali once said: 'One in the eye is worth two in the ear.' While he was referring to boxing, this also applies to making presentations: 'A picture is worth a thousand words.'

Why use visuals?

The average person will remember about 70% of a verbal presentation three hours later and as little as 10% three days later. However, with a visual presentation 85% is remembered three hours later and up to 20% after three days.

Most people's preferred learning style is visual. They need to visualise what you are saying. Make it easy for them by using visuals. Visual support can often make the difference between the audience staying with you or shrugging their shoulders and losing interest.

Use visuals to:

◆ aid retention;
◆ create interest;
◆ illustrate complex material; and
◆ provide variety.

DESIGNING VISUALS

Good design aids your credibility and helps with understanding. If you do not have the time or the skills to create you own audio-visual aids, get somebody to do it for you. Use the communications department, a colleague or a design agency. Keep all visual aids simple and uncluttered (see Figure 4)). Always take along a series of low complexity aids (such as handouts) as a backup. Equipment can fail, so you might want to be prepared to go without audio-visual aids at all.

Avoiding wordy visuals

Words don't made good visuals. Your audience is there to listen to you, not to read from a screen or listen to you reading from a screen. The visuals must enhance your communication with your audience.

> **Be remembered for your message not your slides**.

TECHNIQUES FOR USING VISUAL AIDS

Whenever you show a visual, your audience will stop looking at you and focus on the visual. Be quiet and let your audience look to absorb the information. This is the moment to let the visual do the talking, so don't compete with it.

Be organised. If you are using transparencies, keep them neatly stacked and in the order you are going to use them. Number them discretely, then if you do drop them it will be easy to put them in the order required.

As a rule show only one piece at a time – only as much as you can explain. Go for small self-contained bites. Then add the next piece and comment on it and so on. Don't reveal great chunks of information and then talk. As your commentary unfolds let the visual unfold.

Whiteboards and flipcharts

Flipcharts are excellent to use when you need to record lists of ideas or need to record comments from the audience.

Keep it simple:

◆ Avoid 'bunching' things together.
◆ Leave plenty of unused 'white' space.
◆ Make it big, bold and brilliant.

Keep it organised:

◆ Create a path the eye can follow.
◆ Use arrows and borders.
◆ Justify, centre, etc.

Make something dominant:

◆ The most important element should be immediately obvious.

◆ Highlight the most important element – make use of colour, size, etc.

◆ Use strong, bold colours for lettering.

Text:

◆ Use the landscape position.
◆ Leave a margin on all four sides.
◆ Use punchy phrases rather than sentences.
◆ Five lines maximum.
◆ Five words to a line.
◆ Use pictures to make the point.
◆ Use a uniform typeface.

Fig. 4. Guidelines for designing visual aids.

Pages can be torn from the flipchart and stuck around the room to create an expanding display.

The main drawback of using a whiteboard is the lack of any permanent record of what has been written, unless you are using the electronic whiteboard. These require presentable handwriting to make the best use of them. It is usually best to use block capital letters rather than 'joined up' lettering (see Figure 5).

Handouts

Handouts can be used to develop the key points from your presentation. Ideally, the content should follow the sequence of your presentation and provide detailed information such as

---

Pre-presentation preparation:

◆ Use graphics – cartoons, diagrams – to break up written material.

◆ Cutting corners off preceding pages allows you to locate the prepared sheets.

◆ Leave blank sheets between sections. This allows you to collect ideas from the audience without flipping backwards and forwards.

◆ If you plan to tear off a sheet, score the top with a ruler and make a small cut either side which will ensure a smooth tear.

Before you start:

◆ Check you have enough paper and a spare block.
◆ Check you have pens in various colours.
◆ Ensure the stand is firm and in a good position.

During the presentation:

◆ Avoid writing with your back to the audience.
◆ Keep your display simple – use key words and phrases (not long sentences).
◆ Write in large, clear letters.
◆ Avoid using too many abbreviations.
◆ Emphasise important points by underlining or using colour.
◆ Beware of playing with the marker pen.

Fig. 5. Guidelines for using whiteboards and flipcharts.

research data, evidence, excerpts and other background information (see Figure 6).

♦ Don't cram too much writing on one page.
♦ Use headings, subheadings and paragraphs to break up the text.
♦ Prepare handouts on quality paper.
♦ Check them carefully for accuracy.
♦ Ensure you have one for each member of the audience.
♦ Always tell the audience you will be offering a handout later.

Fig. 6. Guidelines for using handouts.

Overhead projectors (OHPs)

The OHP was once widely used in business presentations but has gradually been replaced by computer-based displays. The main advantage of using an OHP is its ease of use. It requires no warm-up time, there is little or no noise and the only 'searching' is when the presenter looks for the slide he or she wants (see Figure 7).

Before you start:
♦ Take an extension lead if you are unfamiliar with the room.
♦ Ensure a spare bulb is available.
♦ Check the OHP is working.
♦ Focus the OHP.

Positioning the OHP:
♦ Allow the image to fill the screen without overspill.
♦ Keep the screen at right angles to the projector.
♦ Position the screen so the whole audience can see the image.

Where to stand:
♦ The OHP should only be a step or two away from your notes and your transparencies.

◆ If possible, keep transparencies on a separate table – used transparencies can then be easily put out of the way.

◆ Do not stand between the projector and the screen.

Light and noise:

◆ Turn the OHP off at every opportunity – audiences are likely to be distracted by the image on the screen and the noise of the fan.

◆ Adjust the room lighting – if you want the audience to look at you as well as the screen.

◆ Don't make the room too dark.

Avoid:

◆ Talking to the screen.
◆ Leaving the screen illuminated with no image.
◆ Using the pointer as a worry bead!

Fig. 7. Guidelines for using OHPs.

USING COMPUTER-BASED DISPLAYS

Laptop presentations with data projectors are becoming the norm these days. Although the equipment is more complex than an OHP and hence there is more to go wrong, they look professional and modern. They allow a smooth and imaginative transition between slides. The visuals can be sophisticated and incorporate the use of sound and video footage. The presenter can also check the visuals by looking at the laptop and not over his or her shoulder to the screen.

POINTERS FOR USING POWERPOINT

There are lots of features in PowerPoint that allow slide designers to introduce movement and sounds on slides and, unfortunately, these features tend to be overused. Any graphic, sound or video should add value to the point being made, and not there simply because it could be done.

Text movement

Text movement can also cause difficulties. It is difficult to read text as it is moving. The text needs to stop before people can really read it, and this increases the time they are looking at the screen and takes away from the time focused on the presenter. Use text movement with caution.

Dropping into the program

It doesn't look very professional if, during or after the presentation, the audience sees the PowerPoint program displayed on the screen. This happens if you advance past the last slide. You can solve this simply by duplicating your last slide. If you advance one too many it won't matter as the image is the same.

Seeing the slide clearly

So audiences can see the details of your slide clearly, there needs to be a lot of contrast between the text and background colours. A dark blue background with white or yellow text usually works well. Because the text looks good on your computer screen does not mean it will look fine when projected. Most projectors make colours look duller than they appear on a screen. It is always useful to check how the colours look when projected to make sure there is enough contrast.

Pointer showing

It can be distracting for the pointer or little arrow to appear on the screen when the presenter is speaking. To prevent this from happening, after the Slide Show view has started, press the Ctrl+L key combination.

Blank screen

Sometimes you may wish to block the image on the screen completely so you have the attention of the audience. To blank the screen with a black image similar to shutting off the projector, just press the B key on the keyboard. Press the B key again to restore the image. If you want to use a white rather than a black image, press the W key each time.

AID OR DISTRACTION?

Beware of using every bell and whistle available with the software. Mesmerising transitions can distract the audience from your message. People don't come to see a multimedia show: they come to hear what you have to say. You are not there to compete with this wizardry for the audience's attention. It is there to serve you.

The bigger the electronic extravaganza the less significant the presenter can become. The power of Martin Luther King came from his choice of words and how they impacted on people's hearts and minds. He did not need visuals. Visuals are likely to have diluted the power of his words. You may wish to ensure that your visuals aid rather than hinder your message.

SUMMARY

◆ We live in a visual society.

◆ Visuals add interest.

◆ Avoid wordy visuals.

◆ Talk to your audience, not your visuals.

◆ The more complex the equipment, the more can go wrong.

◆ Ensure your visuals are aids, not distractions.

$$4$$

Open and Close with Impact

In this chapter:

◆ getting attention and developing interest
◆ establishing rapport
◆ being credible
◆ how not to open
◆ being humorous
◆ seven ways to open
◆ tips for closing.

GETTING ATTENTION AND DEVELOPING INTEREST

When you stand in front of an audience you have five seconds to get their attention and thirty seconds to develop interest and curiosity. How you open is critical to the success of your presentation. In those opening words you must hook your audience, establish rapport, set the mood, demonstrate your credibility and introduce your topic. Yes, all this in seconds. You cannot afford to waste a moment or 'wing' your opening.

Your opening is your way of 'shaking hands' and building a relationship with your audience. They need to feel good to be meeting you and they need to know you have something useful to say. The opening is less about opening your presentation and more about opening up your audience, so they will be receptive to you and your message.

You cannot afford to make a bad entrance. Otherwise you will waste an opportunity you just won't get again. So hook them with your first sentence. Leave it till the second or third sentence and it will be too late.

What is the likely impact of this opening?

Hello, my name is John Smith and I am here today to talk to you about . . . It is a pleasure to be here . . .

Your opening words must be imaginative, stimulating and attention getting – like those movie posters enticing you to come in to watch the film. This can be followed by your overview – the route map for your presentation. There is no need to give lots of details at this point, just the juicy bits to excite and entice the audience. Like the film-maker, you can also use speed, action, drama, emotion and humour.

ESTABLISHING RAPPORT

Establish rapport with your audience. Let them know you understand how they are thinking and feeling. For example:

Some of you may be thinking you haven't got the time to be sitting here listening to me, but today provides real opportunities . . .

BEING CREDIBLE

Your credibility is likely to be less to do with your academic qualifications and professional experiences and more to do with having a strong posture, quality eye contact and being enthused about your message.

WHAT TO AVOID

Apologising

You may have been asked at the last moment. It may be your first-ever presentation. Never, never, never appeal to the sympathy of your audience:

I was just asked this morning to make this presentation and I haven't had time to prepare.
This is my first time to present . . .

These openings are unhelpful and will undermine your credibility.

Being humorous

One in every one hundred people is good at telling humorous stories, but ten in every one hundred think they are. If you are that one, cultivate this gift and use it. If you are not then beware – your audience may not thank you.

SEVEN WAYS TO OPEN

1. Emphasising the benefits to the audience

Talk people not subject. People buy outcomes not products.

Emphasise what your audience will gain by listening to you:

Today I am going to show you how to do twice as much in half the time

is likely to be far more appealing than:

Today I am going to talk about time management.

2. Telling a story

Stories, especially of those human interest, are generally welcomed by audiences. Make sure your stories are aligned with your objectives and key points, otherwise you risk appearing disjointed.

3. Introducing interesting facts

Begin with an interesting fact that relates to your material. For example:

Eight hours sleep accounts for one third of our day. When translated through a lifetime of 70 years, this amounts to over 23 years. That's a lot of sleep time.

4. Arousing curiosity

Rhetorical questions that demand an answer in your listeners' heads can be a good way to fire the imagination. For example:

What would you do with a million pounds?
Have you ever gone home and said to yourself 'I've had enough'?
Ever lost sales to a competitor you should have beaten but don't know why?

5. Shocking your audience

The internet is going to put us out of business.

6. Using props

Perhaps the easiest way to hold attention is to hold something up for people to look at. For example, hold up a credit card and say:

Imagine life without credit cards.

7. Making topical references

Making reference to a news item, a TV programme or a business issue can be useful as long as they are relevant to your topic and everyone knows what you are talking about.

Your opening words set the tone for your presentation. A shock opening might be great if your want your audience to take action but not if you want them to be relaxed and have some gentle fun. Select your opening to match your objective and remember that no two audiences will react in the same way to the same material.

Suggestion
Collect good openings. As you read newspapers, magazines, listen to other speakers and watch TV, look for ideas that will 'hook' people and record these in a special book.

TIPS FOR CLOSING

Not only is the opening critical to the success of your presentation, so is your conclusion. Prepare your closing and know exactly what you are going to say and do. Create something memorable for the audience to take away with them –

a present, if you like. It needs to be purposeful and memorable and linked to your objectives: to what you want your audience to think, feel and do.

The things to avoid

1. The emergency stop
Here the speaker pulls up in mid-speech to end on time . . . you can almost hear the screech of the brakes as he or she says:

It's 4 o'clock. That's all I have time for. So I'll stop.

This is like someone leaving a conversation suddenly and walking out of the room.

2. You can't get the landing gear down
The speaker can't find the words to end. He or she keeps looping:

I'll finish on that point and remind you of the comment I made earlier about . . .

and off he or she goes again.

The things to do

1. 'Feel-good' ending
Aim for something catchy – a story, a phrase, a thought, an image – that will continue to play in people's minds for hours, days or weeks. This is the time to deliver your take-home message straight to them eye to eye and person to person.

2. The closing summary
The closing summary is useful when the presentation is

intended to convey information and not a call to action:

So we have seen that . . . and this means . . .

3. A call to action

Remind your audience of the benefits of taking action and stir their emotions. Remember, feelings are a catalyst to action.

Beware of padding out your speech to the allotted time. If you finish early most people will consider this a bonus! Rather than overstay your welcome, leave them wanting more. Remember:

◆ Always plan your closing.
◆ Make it catchy, brief and to the point.
◆ Link to the main points of your talk.
◆ Stand confidently and look directly at your audience.
◆ Leave your audience wanting more.
◆ Summarise the main points and answer the question 'now what?'

If your presentation is to be followed by a question and answer session, the impact of your final sentences can be diluted. You can counter this by a second very brief closing after accepting a series of questions.

How you end is how people will remember you. The lasting impression is formed from your final words, be they uplifting and motivating or empty and wishy-washy. Your closing is your signature. You might want to leave your audience feeling upbeat, needed and special.

SUMMARY

◆ A good opening is priceless.

◆ In your opening you must hook your audience, establish rapport and develop credibility.

◆ Never do anything that undermines your credibility.

◆ Collect good openings.

◆ Plan your closing in detail.

◆ Make your last words the things you want your audience to remember.

5

Question and Answer Session

In this chapter:

- ◆ preparing yourself for questions
- ◆ handling questions
- ◆ encouraging questions
- ◆ positioning of the question and answer session.

Many speakers dread the question and answer session, fearing they will be shown up and made to look foolish: 'I may not be able to answer the questions', 'I won't have a script.' However, the question and answer session can be a springboard for you to expand on points that are of interest to your audience. Also, it can help them feel part of the presentation as the exchange is now two-way.

PREPARING YOURSELF FOR QUESTIONS

The professional will anticipate and be prepared to answer any and all questions related to his or her topic. Think about your audience's needs, concerns and interest. Why are they listening to you? What do they want from you? The answers to these questions will indicate the typical questions your audience may ask.

HANDLING QUESTIONS

The people who ask questions range from those who are genuinely confused and need more information, to the person who wants some of the limelight, to the saboteur. You need to be able to distinguish between these and respond appropriately.

ENCOURAGING QUESTIONS

Silence often follows 'Do you have any questions?' Your audience will have its own concerns:

I don't want to look foolish.
My question may not be of interest to the others.
I'm too nervous.
It might be a stupid question.

The following suggestions will make it 'safe' for people to ask questions:

◆ Ask a question yourself: 'A question often asked is . . .'
◆ Adopt a non-threatening, relaxed posture.
◆ Allow time . . . feel OK with silence.
◆ Sip some water.

◆ Put a plant in the audience who will ask the first question and get the ball rolling.

◆ Ask people to discuss with a partner any concerns they have and share these with you. You can then address these concerns – in effect answering their questions.

The question and answer session is for everyone

Listen intently to the questioner and look directly at him or her. Repeat the question in your own words to ensure you understand and everyone else has heard. However, answer not only to the questioner but also to the whole group. Aim to keep your eye contact 20% to the questioner and 80% to the audience. Include them in your comments if appropriate:

I'm sure several of you have come across this problem.

You don't understand the question

At all costs avoid embarrassing the questioner:

You need to make yourself clearer.
I don't understand you.

Try instead:

Help me to understand that a bit more.
Can you say a bit more about that, please?

Keeping to the point

Make your answers short, succinct and to the point. Answer what is asked. Beware of using the question as a springboard to another speech. If they want more information invite them to say so:

Does that answer your question?

You don't know the answer

If you don't know the answer, you may wish to say so. Perhaps it is more important to know where you can find answers than to have all the answers yourself. People are likely to appreciate honesty rather than waste their time listening to you bluff your way through an answer and not fooling anyone: 'I wish I could answer that now but I'd prefer to check some data first.' You may wish to ask if anyone in the audience could help with an answer.

Avoiding argument or long debates

Beware of getting sucked into a discussion that has only limited appeal to your audience. This one-to-one exchange will bore the majority of your audience who will resent being derailed. Recognise what is happening and, in a respectful way, move on:

There is a lot more each of us could add to this debate and I would love to do this at the break, OK?

How to disagree but retain rapport

Keep your voice calm and respect the questioner's right to his or her opinion. Beware of using the 'yes, but . . .' This indicates argument mode and the breaking of rapport.

Always validate the other person's viewpoint before challenging it:

So what you are saying is . . .

Then express your view:

My feelings on this are . . . because . . .
My concerns are . . .

- ◆ Listen carefully to the question.
- ◆ Repeat the question in your own words to ensure you understand and everyone else has heard.
- ◆ If it is a complex question, divide it into parts and state what each is before you answer.
- ◆ Relate your answers to points you have made in your presentation.
- ◆ Answer your question to the whole group.
- ◆ Answer briefly, keeping to the point.
- ◆ Check: 'Does that answer your question?'

Never:

- ◆ Embarrass the questioner.
- ◆ Argue.
- ◆ Be defensive.
- ◆ Bluff.
- ◆ Patronise.
- ◆ Have 'one-to-one' debates.

Fig. 8. Guidelines to answering questions effectively.

POSITIONING THE QUESTION AND ANSWER SESSION

Do you allow questions during your presentation or at the end? There are advantages and disadvantages to both. If you allow questions during your presentation, it can:

- ◆ disrupt the flow of your talk;
- ◆ lose time – answering a question that will be covered later in your talk; and
- ◆ have limited interest – you can get sidetracked by an issue no one else may be interested in.

On the other hand, questions can be valuable feedback for you in terms of where the audience is at and their needs. This allows you to expand on areas of genuine concern.

Never end your presentation with a question and answer session. Follow the question and answer session with a brief summary and then end on a high note with your closing.

SUMMARY

◆ Prepare for questions.

◆ Thinking about your audience's needs and concerns will give you clues to likely questions.

◆ Never embarrass the questioner.

◆ Always maintain rapport.

◆ Answer to the whole group not just the questioner.

◆ Do your closing after the question and answer session.

6

Developing Confidence and Controlling your Nerves

In this chapter:

- ◆ preparing yourself as well as your speech
- ◆ dealing with anxiety
- ◆ visualising success
- ◆ fear is learnt
- ◆ tips for reducing anxiety.

You have prepared your final outline, got your notes together and decided on the visual aids, and now you start thinking about delivering your presentation. Do you get butterflies in your stomach? Sweat a little? Mouth go dry? Are you beginning to panic a bit and it is not even the day of the presentation?

Up to this moment all your preparation has been on the message – what to say and how to say it. Now is the time to concentrate on the messenger, preparing yourself to deliver the message, to create the thoughts and feelings for optimum performance.

PREPARING YOURSELF AS WELL AS YOUR SPEECH

Many great performers in sports and the world of theatre don't perform well unless they experience some stress. Anxiety can give you an edge, make you more alert and give you an energy that makes your presentation sparkling and dynamic. However, you may prefer not to suffer from a dry mouth, sweaty palms, rapid heartbeat or a twitchy stomach.

DEALING WITH ANXIETY

Whatever you feel, you have a strategy for it. Feelings are a consequence of something you do. Your nervousness is related to your thinking. Feelings are less to do with the 'real' world and more to do with what you tell yourself about the 'real' world.

Your teenage son is late. He should have been home from the football game an hour ago. You are worried and anxious because you fear the worst: rival fans fighting each other and your son caught in the middle of it. The more you play the scene in your head, the more vivid you make it, the more blood you see, the more upset you will be. However, your anxious feelings were unfounded. Why? Because at the game he met some school friends and they went to McDonald's for a burger . . . he just never thought of ringing home.

Negative programming

Your mind is like a computer. Programme it with negative messages ('I can't do this', 'I'm no good') and you will get these negative feelings. Like any computer it is obedient and has no other choices than what you programme it with.

VISUALISING SUCCESS

Visualise success. See yourself with good posture and moving confidently as you look out at your audience. Hear yourself speak in a calm, authoritative way. Notice a responsive audience and feel the rapport between you. You feel confident, relaxed and in control. Hear the well deserved applause and people congratulating you on a first-class presentation.

Feed yourself with negative pictures, self-doubts and assumptions of disaster and you will fail:

◆ Eliminate the negative voices.
◆ Recognise what you are good at.
◆ Expect to perform well.
◆ Know you can make a difference.
◆ Care about your audience.

Breaking the cycle of self-doubt

We are often our own worst critics. We can be very good at beating ourselves up and giving ourselves a hard time. Chances are, you are better than you think you are. You might really be that beautiful swan who only thinks he or she is an ugly duckling. You may have yet to discover this as most delegates on my presentation skills courses have. Although reluctant to be video taped, they are surprised and pleased when they see themselves on the TV screen. Typical comments are 'I'm much better than what I thought I was', or 'I didn't come across as nervous'. Seeing how good they really are, rather than the poor presenters they think they are, is a big boost to their self-confidence.

The audience won't expect you to be perfect. *You* might, and then you beat yourself up over those little imperfections that will go unnoticed by your audience.

> **You are better than you think you are.**

Plant flowers not weeds!

My approach to gardening is to plant the flowers so close together that the weeds get smothered and never have a chance to grow. Focus on developing your strengths. Grow flowers in your mind, not weeds. Amplify what is good about you.

You may want to keep a diary of your qualities and add one a day for a month. Ask family and friends what they like about you and why you would make a good speaker. This is not about being superficial and phoney. It is about becoming focused on what you realistically can achieve, growing your strengths, being the best possible you and not allowing the self-doubts appear. As you see yourself in new ways, your feelings will shift. Remember, when you think you are special, you act special.

Anxiety

Anxiety is a software not a hardware problem. It is a question of updating the files we hold on ourselves, and overriding past negative programming with positive self-talk. This may not be as difficult as you think. The human mind can only handle one conscious thought at a time. As simple as it seems, one positive thought might do the trick!

I am sincere
I am intelligent
I have a good sense of humour
I care about my audience
I can make a difference
I have a clear voice
I am creative
I am enthusiastic
I prepare comprehensively
I am . . .
I can . . .
I have . . .

FEAR IS LEARNT

You weren't born afraid of public speaking: it is something you have learnt and it is something you can unlearn. Like most fears it feeds on itself and grows and spreads like a cancer invading many parts of your life. Fear is essentially based on a fantasy, a myth; it is what you run in your head. Really it is:

False
Expectation
About
Reality

You run the pictures of what could go wrong, what you

'know' will go wrong:

◆ I'll dry up.
◆ No one will be interested.
◆ I'll be boring.
◆ I'll lose my place.
◆ My notes will fall on the floor.
◆ My boss lacks confidence in me.
◆ I'll make a show of myself.
◆ They won't like me.
◆ I'm too tall, short, fat.

Plant the flowers of positive expectations and notice the difference. Change the picture in your head and watch the behaviour catch up.

Reversing the symptoms

Rapid breathing, sweating, shaking hands and a high-pitched voice not only reflect your nervousness but also intensify it. Your body takes cues from your mind and your body gives cues to your mind. You control your frame of mind by controlling your body. If you allow yourself to breath rapidly and let your hands shake, your nervousness will grow.

Symptoms of anxiety

Do you do any of the following? If so, reverse these nervous mannerisms if you want to feel more confident:

◆ Pacing aimlessly.
◆ Wringing hands.
◆ Standing cross legged.
◆ Scratching.

◆ Pulling at ear, nose, etc.

◆ Fiddling with keys, coins, jewellery.

◆ Clutching skirt.

◆ Slouching.

◆ Rocking back and forth from heels to toes.

◆ Speaking fast.

◆ Speaking with a high-pitched voice.

Exercise

The next time you do a presentation or even *now*, act as if you were confident. Although it is a bit like the tail wagging the dog, try it and notice the difference:

◆ Hold yourself *now* as if you were confident.
◆ Breath *now* as if you were confident.
◆ Move around *now* as if you were confident.
◆ Gesture *now* as if you were confident.
◆ And so on . . .

Breathing correctly

Breathe slowly and deeply to improve the flow of oxygen into the body and thus the flow of blood to the brain. This will relax you and help you to think more clearly. Taking more oxygen in also improves the flow of air to your vocal chords, allowing you to speak clearly, reducing nervousness and helping you to remain calm.

Getting out of yourself and into your message

You are there to make a difference to your audience. They need to benefit from listening to you. Nerves are often the result of a strong focus on self: '*I* will be boring', 'They won't like *me*'.

Focus on your audience and their needs rather than on yourself. Notice what they might gain and you may not notice your pain. After all, a dog in a hunt doesn't notice it has fleas. Focus on yourself and you will notice the problems. Ask yourself 'How can I make this interesting?' rather than 'Will I look fat wearing this?'

What are you giving your audience?

It might help to imagine the audience needs you or is asking a favour of you. They want information you have, they need your input, they want to tap into your expertise, anything that essentially gives you authority. Recognise that you have genuinely got something the audience needs:

◆ Information.
◆ Life-changing ideas.
◆ Clues to greater profitability.
◆ Solutions to their problems.
◆ Pointers to greater success.
◆ A good time.
◆ A dream to believe in.

TIPS FOR REDUCING ANXIETY

Being prepared

Practise, practise and practise. Rehearse on your own, in front of a mirror, in front of friends. Get so familiar with your material your can deliver it without having to think too much about it. That's when you are likely to be at your best, when you are so familiar with your material that you can concentrate on the audience rather than on yourself or your material.

Start before you start

A professional speaker I know likes to arrive early to an event to socialise with his audience before presenting. He has a coffee, chit chats and generally enjoys their company. This enables him to get to know people and he doesn't feel he is going on cold. He senses he is talking to his friends. He relaxes into his presentation by seeking out these 'friends' in the audience and imagines having a one-to-one conversation with them.

Hiding the shakes

If your hands are inclined to shake, avoid holding notes. When you shake, so does everything you are holding. Find something to set your notes on. Grasp the lectern, table or anything to keep those hands steady.

Playing to your strengths

Concentrate on using your strengths. If you have a good clear voice use it to your advantage. If you have a talent for story-telling, use anecdote. If you can make people laugh, use humour.

Act

Some people are helped by imagining themselves as a famous actor playing the part of a successful, powerful speaker.

Using a checklist

Prepare yourself thoroughly and leave nothing to chance. Use a checklist to ensure you have considered everything (see Appendix 5).

> **Breathing exercise**
> Place one hand on your upper chest and one hand on your diaphragm. Breathe in feeling your diaphragm rise, then breathe out slowly. Repeat several times. The important thing is to feel the diaphragm rise with each intake, not the chest.

Sweating and a dry mouth

If you sweat, you may want to wear a lightweight outfit. If you suffer from a dry mouth, it may help gently to bite the tip of your tongue or imagine yourself sucking a freshly cut lemon.

(Further suggestions for reducing anxiety can be found in Appendix 6.)

SOME THINGS ARE IMPOSSIBLE

Just as it is impossible for the tennis ball to go over the end line if you hit it with good top spin two feet over the net, so you are likely to find it is impossible to be nervous if you are well prepared, breathing deeply, feeling centred and thinking positively.

SUMMARY

◆ Each of us has a strategy for feeling nervous.

◆ We can break the anxiety cycle with positive programming.

◆ Reversing the symptoms of anxiety minimises the feelings.

◆ Focus on your audience rather than on yourself.

◆ Breathing deeply will reduce anxiety.

$$\boxed{7}$$

Your Style of Delivery

In this chapter:

◆ developing presence
◆ posture
◆ gestures
◆ eyes
◆ voice
◆ clothes
◆ the importance of sincerity.

DEVELOPING PRESENCE

Speakers with presence stand tall, move purposefully, connect with their audience, look and sound good. They ooze confidence. How do you come across and how do you communicate presence?

It is suggested that it takes four minutes to form an impression of someone and that 90% of that impression is formed in the first ninety seconds. You don't get a second chance to make a first impression. Make a bad impression and you have lost an opportunity that may never come again.

The following are some guidelines for developing presence and impacting on your audience.

POSTURE: STANDING TALL AND MOVING WITH IMPACT

What does your posture say about you? Do you cross your legs? Do you lean back on one hip, slump, keep your hands in your pockets or fidget?

It is usually best to stand when making a presentation. If you are introduced, you may wish to count to three before you stand to create some anticipation and to give you a sense of control.

Aim to stand upright without being stiff or unnatural. Lengthen your spine, lift your head, drop your shoulders and place your feet shoulder-width apart. Slouching or leaning to one side can make you look over-casual. If you are standing behind a table, avoid leaning on it.

Walk with a sense of purpose rather than pace back and forth as if you were attached to the wall by a thick elastic band.

Confidence is likely to be communicated by fluid, purposeful movements in the body. Nervousness will be indicated by fidgeting, by going back on one hip, by rocking from side to side and by going back and forth on your heels and toes.

Confident people are more likely to lean towards the audience than away from them. It is as if they are keen to get close to the audience to get their message heard. Often the right foot is forward and the right hand gesticulating to the audience.

Avoid:

◆ Hopping from one foot to the other.
◆ Weight on one leg only.
◆ Rocking to and fro.
◆ Swaying.
◆ Going on 'walkabout'.
◆ Standing on the sides of your shoes.

The lectern

Although a lectern can be useful to hold notes and props (and can provide a certain security in your early days as a presenter), the professional speaker usually likes to come out from behind the lectern to have greater impact.

The lectern is often associated with lengthy, tedious droners who talk at us. Standing behind a lectern can make you appear rigid, formal and distant. It is not to be recommended if you want to 'connect' with your audience. It is probably best to use the lectern as a place to put your notes, but stand to the side of it as you speak.

GESTURES: ADDING LIFE AND ENERGY

Gestures add life and colour to your presentation. They can help to paint a picture and will add to the force of your words. In everyday conversation we gesture naturally and are

1. Observe yourself in shops and at home – anywhere there are mirrors. Aim to adopt a stand-tall, confident posture in your everyday life.

2. Sense in your body what walking tall is like. Stand with your heels and shoulders touching the wall and walk away holding that upright posture (you may need to shake a little to avoid being rigid). Register this feeling in your body and replicate this before a presentation.

3. Another quick and easy way to stand tall is to stand upright and close your eyes. Allow your head to fall backwards as far as is comfortably possible. Now drop your head forward as far as is comfortably possible and bring your head back so your eyes are looking straight ahead. Now open your eyes and you will have a stand-tall posture.

4. Imagine a string from the middle of the top of your head pulling you upwards, and notice how tall you can walk and feel.

5. Rather than continuously move as you present, aim to talk from different locations. Having presented centre stage, move a few steps to the right and present from that spot. Repeat this so you make several location shifts during your presentation.

6. Get a friend to 'sculpt' you into a high credibility posture. Pay attention to how this feels and adjust your body so you feel even more confident.

7. Video yourself making a presentation and review this with people whose comments you value.

8. Notice people on TV, at conferences, in meetings, who impress you with their posture.

Fig. 9. Tips for developing good posture.

probably not aware of them. When you present, aim to gesture as you would in an animated conversation with a friend – nothing more. With a large group your gestures and energy may need to be 'larger than life', just as the statue on top of a building needs to be of a larger than life size to appear of life-like proportions to an onlooker from the ground. Gestures that are too bold will only distract. If you are inclined to over-gesture, it may help to keep your elbows by your side with hands held slightly in front.

Your hands do not have a separate identity. They are an extension of your arms and only need to move if you are making a gesture. It is OK to keep your hands empty and still by the sides of your body. This may feel odd to you but will look natural from the audience's view. Observe people on TV and how they hold their hands. There is no need to keep the hands glued to your sides. Experiment and find something that is comfortable for you – perhaps one hand holding notes leaving the other free to gesture or your hands held slightly in front at waist level gesturing naturally.

What not to do with your hands:

◆ Fidget with rings, coins or the pointer.
◆ Put them behind your back.
◆ Have them folded across your chest.
◆ Put them in your pockets.
◆ Scratch.

EYES: CONNECTING WITH YOUR AUDIENCE

Eye contact is like an electric current that keeps audiences tuned in and connected to you. Turn off the current and you disconnect their involvement. If you don't pay attention to your audience, they will find it difficult to pay attention to you.

Steady, direct eye contact communicates honesty, warmth

and authority. Eye contact is essential. When there is eye contact, a highly personal exchange takes place. It is with your eyes that you 'connect' with your audience and keep their interest.

Good eye contact is not a fleeting glance; nor is it sweeping your gaze back and forth across an audience like some form of human searchlight. Look into people's eyes as if you are having a one-to-one conversation. This usually involves keeping eye contact for five to ten seconds before moving on to another person. It may help to imagine you are giving that person a little present, a present of information, and you want that person to feel special, to feel you are actually talking to him or her.

In a large audience when you look at one person, people in the vicinity of that person will also feel you are talking just to them. In a large group talk to individuals all over the room as a way of making everyone feel the presentation belongs to them. Keep your head up and vary the direction of your gaze.

Nervous people are likely to want to look anywhere but at the audience. The ceiling, the floor, the screen all become more preferable than the terrifying prospect of looking into some-one's eyes. As a rule, aim to speak to someone all the time, accepting that you may need to break eye contact to look at your notes, pick up a prop or read a passage.

Think twice about handing out props or handouts. You might be competing with them for the eyes and interest of your audience.

Some dos and don'ts

Do:

◆ Make eye contact with individual members of your audience.

◆ Imagine you are giving this person a present of information.

◆ Move your gaze to individuals in different parts of the room.

◆ Involve everyone equally.

Don't:

◆ Talk to the floor, ceiling or screen.

◆ Scan the room from side to side.

◆ Avoid eye contact with people you perceive to be negative.

◆ Focus only on the 'friendly' people in your audience.

---

1. Observe presenters on TV, at conferences and in meetings and note how they make eye contact, for how long and how this impacts on the audience.

2. Practise keeping steady eye contact for 5–10 seconds with people in everyday conversations.

3. Here is a little exercise for you to practise the 5–10 second rule with a small group of people. Ask them to each raise three fingers. Each person is to lower one of their fingers each time you make eye contact with that person for 5–10 seconds. Present to this group on a topic that is easy for you to talk about.

4. Video yourself and observe your eye contact patterns.

Fig. 10. Tips for improving eye contact.

VOICE: DEVELOPING A CONVERSATIONAL TONE

Your voice is the vehicle you use to convey your message. You can have an 'old banger' that rattles along or a smooth, finely tuned Rolls-Royce. You may have the most fascinating and radical ideas but, if you present in a dull, flat, monotone way, your audience is likely to turn off and not hear those life-changing ideas.

To encourage a conversational voice, use notes or a story-board – anything that just triggers off ideas for you to talk to your audience about. This not only allows you to appear professional but also allows your personality to shine through.

When you are nervous, your breathing is shallow and the muscles in the throat tense. The voice is deprived of its power and range and loses animation. Deepen the breathing to provide fuel for the voice.

A keyboard that plays only one note is not easy on the ear. Add interest to your voice by varying the tone, pace and volume. Speak softly or slow down for emphasis. This is a bit like verbal highlighting. By using your full range of vocal 'notes' you will be easier to listen to.

When you want to impress deeply on your audience, you may want to look directly into their eyes and pause. This has the same effect as a sudden and loud noise: it attracts attention and people are more alert to what you have to say next.

Some dos and don'ts

Do:

- Speak in a conversational way.
- Vary your voice in volume and emphasis.
- Change the pace.
- Pause.
- Speak clearly and in a controlled way.
- Allow time for the sound of your voice to travel in a large room.

Do not:

- Rush.
- Speak in a monotone way.

If you dry up:

- Sip some water.
- Imagine the juice of a lemon in your mouth.
- Gently bite your tongue to generate saliva.

CLOTHES: DRESSING FOR SUCCESS

Clothes don't just cover the body – they communicate and provide a self-portrait of you. What you wear tells your audience something about how you feel about yourself and how you feel about this group. Shirts and blouses speak volumes: colours make announcements and shoes talk. Dress to convey confidence and credibility, and you may want to dress in clothes that allow you to feel good.

1. Listen to people who have interesting voices and analyse them.

2. To create variety in your voice, imagine your audience is blind or there is a curtain between you. You are totally dependent on your voice to communicate energy and feeling.

3. Record yourself and listen to your voice critically. This may be a presentation you give or you could even leave a mini-speech message on your voice mail.

4. Ask a friend to listen to you talk with his or her eyes closed, as if he or she were hearing your voice over the radio. How would your friend describe your voice? What is the image your voice projects? And so on.

5. Visit a speech coach for a series of lessons to improve articulation and variety.

6. Practise diaphragmatic breathing.

Fig. 11. Tips for developing an interesting voice.

THE IMPORTANCE OF SINCERITY: NEVER SAY ANYTHING YOU DON'T BELIEVE IN

Why? Because the audience will know. People have a sixth sense – they will be sensitive to those subtle changes (that you probably won't notice) to voice tone, to your eyes and to your body that lets them know how you are feeling. Something inside of them will tell them you are lying, giving a sales pitch, nervous or your smile is phoney. Always assume your audience will know.

KEEPING IT SIMPLE

Rather than plan your gestures, pauses, movements and smiles, let it all come from your heart, out of your belief and enthusiasm for your topic. Believe:

◆ in what you have to say;

◆ your audience will benefit from listening to you; and

◆ that you can make a difference.

Now you will pause, gesture and move naturally. An ounce of spontaneity is worth a ton of rules. Your speaking persona is not something you can put on like a dinner jacket.

SUMMARY

◆ You don't get a second chance to make a first impression.

◆ Confident people stand tall and move purposefully.

◆ Gesture as you would in an animated conversation.

◆ Keep eye contact with your audience and they will keep contact with you.

◆ Speak in a conversational way.

◆ Dress to aid your credibility.

◆ Speak from your heart and you will do a lot of things right.

(8)

Never be Boring Again

In this chapter:

◆ wrapping your presentation
◆ keeping the interest of your audience
◆ attention span
◆ making your presentation brain friendly
◆ whole-brain wrapping
◆ the importance of picture language
◆ ways to aid retention.

You can barely stay awake. You stifle yet another yawn. You can't remember the points made by the speaker. You long for the end. And yet the speaker is well prepared, has style, enthusiasm and energy. He is eloquent, with great posture and a clear voice. Why is he not impacting on the audience?

Giving a presentation is like giving someone a present. The present (your content), the wrapping paper (structure of message), and the giving (delivery style) all dovetail to make the presentation experience. A shallow message, a poor delivery, a conceited personality or a badly structured message will spoil the experience for your audience.

People are inclined to put most of their efforts into the content of their presentation with some thought for the delivery. Often the wrapping is neglected.

DOES THE WRAPPING MATTER?

You may have a life-enhancing message but if it is not wrapped appropriately, you will not be 'heard' and you won't be changing any lives. It is not just a matter of what you say – how you structure your ideas also matters. To decide on the 'wrapping paper' for your ideas, you need to understand people and something of the psychology of communication.

How do you present so people:

◆ Stay interested?
◆ Remain open to your ideas?
◆ Enjoy the experience?
◆ Take action?

KEEPING THE INTEREST OF YOUR AUDIENCE

In today's society we are bombarded by information. Our attention span seems to be getting shorter due to the influence of the media. We are accustomed to getting information quickly, in small doses and in stimulating ways. The people in your audience have come to expect this.

Everything is at a much faster pace: instant food, instant gratification and instant information. The pace of life has changed and presenters need to match this or be 'fast-forwarded'.

You risk losing interest if you:

◆ Don't hook the audience in the opening seconds.
◆ Don't get right to the point.
◆ Dwell too long on any one point.
◆ Provide too much detail.
◆ Fail to make your presentation visual.
◆ Fail to involve your audience.
◆ Fail to have a variety of presentation methods.

> **Add variety to sustain your audience's interest.**

Variety wrapping

Variety is the spice of your speaking life. To keep the interest and attention of your audience, you must do something different, frequently. Look around the room you are in and select an object to concentrate on. How long before your mind switches to something else or to another thought? To hold your attention, the object needs to flash, move, or change in some way, etc., every 20–30 seconds. So if you want the listener to continue to pay attention to you, add variety ever 20–30 seconds.

Self-interest wrapping

Juries remember only 60% of what they are told. Why? The case is not about them. No matter how hard they try, people have difficulty paying attention to presentations that aren't about them.

Suggestions

◆ Change the pace.
◆ Increase energy.
◆ Introduce props.
◆ Show a visual.
◆ Use metaphor.
◆ Involve the audience.
◆ Ask a rhetorical question.
◆ Use a movie clip.
◆ Be humorous.
◆ Be dramatic.
◆ Tell a story.
◆ Use a sound clip.
◆ Be emotional.
◆ Share a personal experience.
◆ Use suspense.
◆ Use colour.
◆ Pause.

People are primarily interested in themselves. They want to know how to earn more money, how to live longer, how to get cheaper holidays, how to get promotion and so on. Talk to the self-interest of your audience. Talk about them, their problems and their concerns. The more times you can add the words 'you' or 'yours' the more interest you create for your audience. While it is your presentation, it is all about *them* and for *them*.

Good presenters do it in less time

Radio and television news make use of the thirty-second 'sound bite', as it is sometimes called. It takes thirty seconds for the story, which might include an interview with an eye-witness and pictures of the news event. Every few seconds there is a change of scene.

30-second 'bite' wrapping

You can make powerful messages in thirty seconds. Your presentation can be a series of mini-presentations made up of thirty-second bites. The following questions can form the basis for a presentation proposal. If you want a fast-moving presentation, aim to answer each of these questions in thirty seconds or less:

◆ Where are we now?
◆ How did we get here?
◆ Where are we going?
◆ Why are we going there?
◆ What are the obstacles?
◆ What are the options?
◆ The proposed solution?
◆ Benefits of this option?
◆ Costs if we don't run with this?
◆ Outline an implementation plan.
◆ Call for action.

While it might not be appropriate to answer each question in thirty seconds, you might want to aim for the thirty-second mindset. Rather than bore your audience with detail, make the key points jump right out in thirty-second bites and put the details on a handout.

This approach disciplines the mind and tightens the message. It enables you to sharpen rather than suffocate the issues as ideas can get lost when there is an abundance of words:

◆ Get right to the heart of the matter.
◆ Be concise and move on.
◆ Make points clearer by deleting, not adding, words.

ATTENTION SPAN

People can speak on average 150 words per minute but the human mind can process approximately 400 words per minute. This means the people listening to you have spare mental capacity. If this is not engaged, your audience will drift off and daydream.

How do you involve more of the person? How do you make your message come alive and get your audience to see, hear and feel what you are saying? How do you engage that spare capacity?

MAKING YOUR PRESENTATION BRAIN FRIENDLY

In a moment I'd like you to think of a happy memory, something that allows you to feel good. It could be a recent memory or one from your distant past. Take a few moments and, when you have found such a memory, just relive the moment. Be there in your mind, explore the place, notice who is there and see the colours. Pay attention to the sounds and let the feelings come. Give yourself time to do this, now.

Did you have that memory as a picture? Most people think in pictures. Each of us has a bio-computer in our heads on which we project our memories. Some of us will have colour screens, others black and white. It is not as if one is better than another, just different.

Some of us have multimedia systems – we get sounds as well as pictures. Can you hear your Mum's voice in your head or your favourite piece of music? I suspect many of you will have been able to get some feelings as you replayed the memory.

So each of us has an optimum way of having memories and taking on new information. Do you seem to get more out of a presentation when there are lots of visuals, stories and demonstrations? Or are you the sort who likes to listen to the material and sometimes gets 'lost' in the notes? Or do you do best with interactivity and hands on?

The vast majority of your audience will be visual dominant, followed by feeling people and the least represented will be the auditory. My work with people indicates that up to 60% of people are visual dominant, 30% kinaesthetic and only 10% auditory.

What are the implications?

The presenter needs to communicate with the audience in ways that match the preferred thinking style of the audience. Otherwise it is a bit like speaking on a different frequency and you will be on a different wavelength.

To hold the group's attention and keep its interest, make the presentation predominantly visual and kinaesthetic. Boring presentations are likely to be too auditory: people just cannot make pictures in their heads of what is being said.

Acetates full of text are in the auditory mode. Even a picture slide is static – it is less engaging than the pictures people make in their heads when you talk metaphors and anecdotes:

◆ *Visual* people learn best by demonstration and modelling. They like to see and be shown.

◆ *Auditory* people learn best by hearing, reading and being told.

◆ *Kinaesthetic* people learn best by 'having a go'. They like 'hands on' involvement and activity.

WHOLE-BRAIN WRAPPING

To be effective as a communicator use all three systems. This multi-sensory approach involves more of the brain and, hence, learning is more effective, retention is enhanced and spare capacity is utilised (see Figure 12).

THE IMPORTANCE OF PICTURE LANGUAGE

When you hear words like 'baby', 'Wimbledon' or 'alligator', what comes up on your bio-computer? Now hear words like 'philosophy', 'process', 'perception'. Which words did you see in your imagination? Use picture words to retain interest and to help your audience to listen and stay with you.

Rather than say there is a famine in Africa, describe what it looks, feels and sounds like when helpless children starve to death. In this way you will transform dry facts into pictures people will relate and react to.

Aim to use words that paint a picture your audience will never forget. By relating to your own and your audiences' personal experiences, you can touch the minds and hearts of your audience. Illustrate with personal stories and reach the hearts of your listeners so they can see, feel and touch what you are saying. As you prepare your words ask:

What will my audience see in their imaginations if I say this?

> Cold facts are not the stuff of which eloquence is fashioned.

If you have a technically minded audience and you are presenting the results of some research, it is appropriate to use

Visuals:

◆ Use pictures, graphs, charts, photographs and slides – anything that has a visual impact.

◆ Invite the audience to imagine, to see in their minds' eyes.

◆ Tell stories and use metaphors and anecdotes.

◆ Dress for success – your credibility will be linked to how you look.

◆ Use words like 'Is that clear to you?', 'Let me show you', 'Can you see that?'

Auditory:

◆ Talk about successes in other contexts.

◆ Vary the pitch, tone and volume of your voice.

◆ Pay as much attention to how you say it as to what you say.

◆ Use play on words (e.g. puns).

◆ Use words like 'Does that sound good to you?', 'I'd like to amplify this point'.

Kinaesthetic:

◆ Get them involved with your ideas.

◆ Let them trial the proposal before making a firm decision.

◆ This type needs to feel comfortable with you and, indeed, be sitting comfortably.

◆ They like to touch such things as props or a brochure.

◆ 'How do you feel about this idea?' 'How would you be more comfortable with it?' 'Raise your hands those who agree.'

◆ They need hands-on activities – small group or pair work.

◆ Ask rhetorical questions to involve them: 'So what is the answer to this dilemma?' 'So what is the way forward?'

Fig. 12. Guidelines for whole-brain wrapping.

abstract language. However, you extend your range of appeal if you combine picture language with the technical data.

Restating numbers in visual ways

Nine and a half thousand pedestrians are killed in accidents each year in Europe. That is the equivalent of six Boeing 737 planes crashing every month killing all the passengers. That is one disaster every five days.

Your legs will carry you over 70,000 miles in your lifetime, almost three times around the world!

Proverbs are almost all visual sayings, which make them easy to remember and act on. The similes that have been passed on for centuries are also visual:

Flat as a pancake.
Sly as a fox.
As hard as a rock.

You may speak very eloquently with good posture and clear voice but you will not impact if you don't use picture language and involve your audience.

Picture-building words

The speaker who is easy to listen to sets colourful, dynamic images floating before our eyes. The person who uses foggy, abstract, colourless words sets the audience nodding. Sprinkle pictures throughout your talk. The picture words just leap up, almost as if they are smiling at you, before going scampering off and feeding the imagination of your audience. A novel you just cannot put down has become a vivid dynamic movie in your head. You, too, will be a captivating speaker if you stir the imaginations and touch the hearts of the audience. This is the secret of people who are considered charismatic.

> **The best pictures are on the radio!**

BE BORING AND BE ZAPPED!

People today are used to channel surfing – flicking backwards and forward through the TV channels, searching for interesting programmes. If your presentation lacks variety, is not visual or involving, you will be boring and the audience would probably love to fast-forward the presentation. However, they will probably just change channels by day-dreaming.

Beware of creating a passive audience. Look at people who fall asleep in front of the TV despite the noise. This is because they are inactive and uninvolved, which leads to lowered energy and disinterest.

People forget fast

People forget 40% of what was said within twenty minutes of hearing your presentation. Within half a day, they lose 60% and, within one week, 90% of it is gone.

No matter how well delivered and entertaining your presentation, most of what you will say will be quickly forgotten. Aim to capture the essence of your message in a way that makes it easy to remember and act on after your presentation. A clever take-away slogan will help to make your key point more memorable in the minds of your listeners.

We remember best what is:

- First and last in a session.
- Repeated.
- Outstanding or different.
- Visual.
- Emotional.

People remember:

- 10% of what they *read.*
- 20% of what they *hear.*
- 30% of what they *see* done.
- 50% of what they *read, hear* and *see* done.
- 70% of what they *read, hear, see* done and *explain* to someone else.
- 90% of what they *read, hear, see* done, *explain* and *do* themselves.

Words that get attention

Here is a selection of words that seem to grab people's attention. Use them to inject verbal energy into your presentation:

- success
- proven
- amazing
- discover
- learn
- how to
- free
- new
- exciting
- guarantee
- results
- best.

Energy phrases

The following phrases similarly inject verbal energy into your presentation:

◆ Three ways to . . .
◆ Shortcuts to . . .
◆ Be an expert on . . .
◆ Secrets of . . .
◆ Smart solutions to . . .
◆ Four tips on . . .
◆ Solve . . .
◆ Transform . . .
◆ Achieve . . .
◆ Overcome . . .
◆ Five steps to . . .

Non-words

Generally speaking, avoid jargon and clichés:

◆ 'I hear what you are saying'.
◆ 'Not to put too fine a point on it'.
◆ 'And without further ado'.
◆ 'Better safe than sorry'.

Talking in positive terms

Have you ever noticed when you go on a diet and decide not to eat chips and cream cakes what it is you become obsessed with? Yes those chips and cream cakes just won't leave your mind.

The mind does not seem to be able to handle negatives except as positives. For example, 'Don't think of a pink elephant' and what do you get? Yes, a pink elephant. The human mind seems to need to create the elephant first and then erase it.

If you phrase things in negative terms to your audience, you may just communicate the opposite of what you want to achieve:

◆ 'I'm not here to sell to you'.
◆ 'I don't want us to fall out over this'.
◆ 'This is going to be difficult'.

Keep the focus on what you want rather than on what you don't want. Otherwise it will be like the golfer who says to him or herself as they are about to strike the ball 'I don't want to hook the ball'. The chances are he or she will hook the ball precisely because of what they are telling themselves. Keep the focus of your audience on what you want rather than on what you don't want.

Rule of three

There is a rhythm of three, which seems to work well in speaking. The most powerful and influential phrases of history reflect this grouping of three:

> *Of the people, by the people and for the people.*
> *Never in the field of human conflict was so much owed by so many to so few.*

The Preface to this book uses this rule of three, and you may find it will add to the strength and power of your spoken words.

SUMMARY

◆ To impact on your audience, pay attention to the wrapping for your ideas.

◆ Add variety to sustain the interest of your audience.

◆ Powerful messages can be made in thirty-second bites.

◆ You may have to give people dry information but there is no need to make a dull presentation.

◆ Use picture words and involve the audience if you don't want to be boring.

◆ People remember what is first and last in a session.

◆ Draw the attention of the audience to what you want rather than what you don't want.

◆ The rule of three will add power to your words.

$$9$$

Which Planet is your Audience from?

In this chapter:

◆ matching your style of delivery to the needs of the audience
◆ understanding the four main personality types
◆ guidelines for presenting to go-getters
◆ guidelines for presenting to carers
◆ guidelines for presenting to analyticals
◆ guidelines for presenting to socialisers.

DIFFERENT PEOPLE WANT DIFFERENT THINGS

Pete wants the presentation to be short, snappy and to the point. Erika likes to 'connect' with the speaker and wants the presentation to be personal. On the other hand, Susanne wants it detailed, structured and precise. Leroy wants it to be fun and entertaining and the presenter to be enthusiastic. To be successful, somehow the presenter must connect with Pete, Erika, Susanne and Leroy's different styles.

There is no one style of presenting, which will be good for everyone in the audience. Often we fall into the trap of thinking that the way I like to be presented to is the best way to present. While your style is good, it will not always be appropriate. Not everyone wants the presentation to be short, snappy and to the point. A giant step in improving your effectiveness will be to recognise the dominant style of the group and adapt to this.

The following is a brief overview of the four main personality types with guidelines for customising your presentation to each. The difference between people is not minor – it is dramatic, it is as if we are from different planets.

UNDERSTANDING THE FOUR MAIN PERSONALITY TYPES

Go-getters (Pete)

These are assertive, high-energy, no-nonsense people who love to achieve and get things done. They have a direct style, call a spade a spade and sound as if they mean what they say. They are inclined to use absolutes ('This will never work') and are inclined to tell rather than ask.

Communication is often a one-way affair. They are inclined to be functional and get in touch only when they want something. They have little time for small talk and like their information concise, 'one-minute-manager' style. Bullet points often characterise this style. They are inclined to talk bottom line and ways to obtain better results. They won't appreciate their time 'wasted' by long, drawn-out stories.

For these people less is better. Stand up, speak up, shut up and finish early. If you are including notes of your presentation, make sure there is a one-page summary, preferably with bullet points.

Go-getters are often found in audiences of salespeople, senior mangers and entrepreneurs.

Some dos and don'ts

Do:

◆ Get straight to the heart of the matter.
◆ Speak with authority and confidence.
◆ Be brief and to the point.
◆ Use bullet points.
◆ Talk benefits and solutions.
◆ Give them useful tips and techniques, anything that makes their lives easier.
◆ Be time conscious.
◆ Be positive and dynamic.
◆ Make strong eye contact and use forceful gestures.
◆ Make it 'punchy'.

Don't:

◆ Spend long on the introduction.
◆ Pad out time.
◆ Be indirect.
◆ Nitpick.

◆ Give 'chapter and verse'.
◆ Be problem focused.
◆ Start late or overrun.
◆ Overload on detail or long explanations.

Carers (Erika)

These are warm, sincere, sensitive people who are good listeners and who value quality relationships. They like to 'connect' with people. Small talk is seen as a way to bond with others. They are naturally interested in people and ask open questions of others.

They shy away from conflict and generally want to please. They are not demanding and have an indirect style of communicating. They are usually quietly spoken and have soft, rounded gestures. They avoid drawing attention to themselves and are generous in their praise of others.

Carers need to connect with the presenter, so information of a personal nature will be appreciated. They need to see the presenter as a genuine, sincere person. They will want to feel 'safe' with you and won't want to be singled out and certainly not 'belittled' in any way.

Carers are often found in audiences of nurses, social workers, counsellors and teachers.

Some dos and don'ts

Do:
◆ Make it personal.
◆ Be empathetic.

◆ Be responsive to the needs of the audience.
◆ Be sincere.
◆ Use stories of human interest.
◆ Show the real you.
◆ Make it interactive.
◆ Be friendly.
◆ Have a 'chatty' conversational style.
◆ Talk feelings.

Don't:

◆ Put your audience down.
◆ Talk at the audience.
◆ Pick on an individual.
◆ Be in their face.
◆ Argue.
◆ Be sarcastic.
◆ Be cynical.

Analyticals (Susanne)

These people are analytical, logical, rational, principled and are driven to get things right. They strive for perfection and like order, structure and procedures. They think before they speak and are conservative by nature. They speak in a deliberate, controlled way with little inflection or expression to the voice. They tend to be formal and distant with few facial expressions.

As presenters, they like to deal with facts rather than opinions or human-interest stories. Their energy is low and they are inclined to present lots of information, which has been thoroughly researched. They may even overrun on time to ensure the audience has all the relevant data. They will appreciate detailed handouts to read at their leisure after the presentation.

Your credibility is linked to how you demonstrate your knowledge of your subject and to presenting this in a logical, structured way. You are likely to be taken more seriously if you mention the problems up front and deal with them as part of your presentation.

Analyticals are often found in audiences where there are accountants, engineers, systems analysts and computer programmers.

Some dos and don'ts

Do:

◆ Be structured.
◆ Provide an overview and stick to it.
◆ Make your case in a logical, ordered way.
◆ Provide proof and data.
◆ Give lots of supportive evidence.
◆ Cover all the aspects.
◆ Notice problems and difficulties.
◆ Keep your energy low.
◆ Be serious.
◆ Provide lots of statistics.
◆ Provide detailed handouts.
◆ Deal with facts rather than opinions.
◆ Be accurate.
◆ Be unemotional.

Don't:

◆ Talk feelings.
◆ Be interactive.
◆ Exaggerate or overstate.
◆ Use superlatives.
◆ Jump from idea to idea.
◆ Plead or use emotional blackmail.
◆ Show a slide with even the smallest mistake.

Socialisers (Leroy)

These are fairly easy-going, open-minded people who like to experiment and to try new ways of doing things. They like variety and there can be surprises when they present.

They are inclined to communicate in an enthusiastic, dramatic way with lots of inflection in the voice. They share feelings and stories and they like to hear the opinions of others. They are inclined to use superlatives. They bore easily and like variety. Generally they want an easy-going, fun relationship with the speaker and want the presentation to be entertaining as well as informative.

Entertainers are often found in audiences of people who have glamorous, high-profile jobs: entertainers, public relations and TV people.

Some dos and don'ts

Do:

◆ Perform.
◆ Make it fun.
◆ Use variety.

◆ Be enthusiastic.
◆ Make it different.
◆ Change the pace and style frequently.
◆ Make it interactive.
◆ Provide options.
◆ Be imaginative.

Don't:

◆ Be boring.
◆ Use lots of statistics.
◆ Talk at the audience.
◆ Be long.

In your audience you are likely to have a mix of these personality types. With select groups you are likely to have a dominant type (e.g. the majority of salespeople are likely to be go-getters). You could expect most accountants to be analyticals and nurses to be mainly carers.

Your success as a presenter comes from noticing the dominant type of your audience and matching your presentation style to this, even if it is uncomfortable for you. Because something is uncomfortable does not mean it is wrong, it just means you haven't being doing it regularly. Successful people do the uncomfortable. This is one of the reasons why they are successful. Stay within your comfort zone and you limit your success. Experiencing discomfort could be a sign you are taking yourself to the next level.

SUMMARY

◆ Your audience will be made up of different personality types.

◆ Go-getters will want you to be short, snappy and to the point.

◆ Carers will want to 'connect' with you.

◆ Analyticals will want you to be detailed, structured and precise.

◆ Socialisers will want you to be entertaining and enthusiastic.

◆ Take your presenting to the next level by matching your style to the needs of your audience.

10

Fishing with Chicken Vindaloo?

In this chapter:

◆ the presenter is a salesperson
◆ logic does not always persuade
◆ the secret of selling
◆ persuading the personality types
◆ developing flexibility.

Speakers are often sales people. They need to persuade their audience, they need them to buy their ideas, support their proposal and take action. How do you get people to 'buy' your information, product, ideas or solution?

Without realising it, many of us attempt to influence in the way we like to be persuaded, using *my* strategy and values instead of the other person's strategy. This is a bit like fishing with chicken vindaloo. I like chicken vindaloo, but I'm not likely to catch many fish using it as bait! The person who is persuaded by logic is likely to present in a logical, structured way.

LOGIC DOES NOT ALWAYS PERSUADE

Reason is probably the most common persuasion tactic among business people: putting forward a rational, logical case. However, reason alone for some people is not sufficient. Decision-making is not always rational and objective. People can see the logic of a proposal but their heart will tell them something different.

> **The heart has its reasons, which are quite unknown to the head**
> *(Blaise Pascal).*

THE SECRET OF SELLING

The man who invented the vacuum cleaner went bankrupt. He sold the patent to a Mr Hoover who brought his new-fangled electric broom to department store buyers. They turned it down. There was no need for this contraption. People bought inexpensive brooms to clean floors and rugs. Who would want to spend more money for an electrical gadget that did the same job?

A want was created by a clever marketing person. Mr Hoover's sales force went into homes spilling dirt on rugs and whisking them clean with his new vacuum cleaner. It wasn't long before every home had to have one.

Creating the need

If you create a need, people will buy. It is easier to sell fences after a storm. It is easy to sell pills when someone has a headache. Make it easy for people to buy your ideas by creating a need first.

People selling burglar alarms may grow the need by talking about the number of recent break-ins in the neighbourhood and only then mentioning their product and what it can do for the householder.

Growing the need

Grow the need if you don't want to appear 'pushy' or to be giving a hard sell. Talk in visual ways about:

◆ rising costs;
◆ lengthening delays;
◆ losing market share;
◆ falling profits; and
◆ increased staff turnover.

You introduce the need for change by showing why the present situation should not continue. Express this as vividly as you can and tease out the consequences. In this way you will grow the need for change. It is like digging the hole in which you will plant your idea or proposal.

See yourself as a want-creator rather than a need-filler. You are not so much selling a solution as creating the need. The stronger you create the need, the more people will want to buy your ideas.

Influencing is complex

Here are some other factors to consider in getting agreement:

◆ Build rapport.
◆ Establish trust.
◆ Demonstrate your credibility.
◆ Show you care.
◆ Talk benefits.
◆ Tell them what they lose by not buying.
◆ Appeal to feelings, values and beliefs.

PERSUADING THE PERSONALITY TYPES

Go-getters

You raise their interest level if you emphasise benefits to them rather than features. Zoom in on bottom-line results with brief benefit statements. Talk increased productivity, saved time, profits and efficiency. Emphasise 'hassle-free' service rather than personal loyalty.

Show how you can take them to the next level and be leaders in their field rather than be second best with competitors taking the advantage.

Some points to consider

To create rapport with and to persuade go-getters you should:

◆ Show how you can support their goals.
◆ Give recognition to their ideas.
◆ Be candid and direct.
◆ Avoid heated debate – they are likely to want to win.
◆ Make sure they hear a benefit for them.
◆ Be efficient rather than nice.

- Make it challenging.
- Tell them how they will be rewarded.
- Make it high status.
- Introduce a competitive element.

Go-getter presenters often lose rapport with other types by overstating benefits and countering objections too forcefully. They are inclined to push too early for the close and to show impatience with indecision.

Carers

Take a soft gentle approach. Give your proposal a 'people-benefit' frame. Talk about how this will enhance people's lives and relationships. Offer continuous support and partnership. Show you need their help and then ask for that help.

It is critical the presenter comes across as genuine and trustworthy, otherwise there is likely to be resistance to your ideas. They 'buy' the person. If they like you they are more likely to be open to your ideas. Avoid the 'hard-sell' and offer personal guarantees.

Some points to consider

To create rapport with and to persuade carers you should:

- Make suggestions and recommendations rather than go into any form of telling.
- Validate their concerns and feelings.
- Stay engaged with them personally.
- Offer support and avoid any form of pressure.
- Show how people problems can be solved.

◆ Talk about improving the quality of relationships.

◆ Show how you can aid harmony and reduces stress or conflict.

◆ Link your ideas to people benefits.

When presenting, carers need to be on guard against understating benefits and sounding unconvincing in answering objections. Also, they can be hesitant to ask for the close.

Analyticals

You don't persuade, your data does. They will 'buy' the argument not the person. Give them lots of information about your product and its features and let them make up their own minds. Talking benefits can come across to analyticals as a 'hard sell'.

Give them logical proof from reliable sources. Be risk averse. It is best to present the 'new' as an extension of the old and proven. Discounts and special offers do little for analyticals.

Quality is very important to these people, and they like value for money. *Not* is often a good word – 'This is *not* expensive', 'This is *not* high risk.'

Some points to consider

To create rapport with and to persuade analyticals you should:

◆ Have an organised and thoughtful approach.

◆ Give lots of information.

◆ Provide guarantees.

◆ Avoid gimmicks.

◆ Restate the big picture to prevent getting lost in the detail.

◆ Talk about risk free.

◆ Mention standards, quality and the need to get things right.

◆ Show you have double checked.

◆ Talk systems and schedules.

Analyticals often present with so much detail that the audience becomes confused. Generally they expect the data to do the persuading and are inclined to outline features without emphasising benefits. They don't always see the need for rapport with their audience.

Socialisers

Be enthusiastic about your proposal. Sell the 'sizzle' as well as the steak! Be upbeat, friendly and lively. They are likely to want a sense of partnership and working together.

Your enthusiasm for your ideas will help to persuade. Talk about something new, different and innovative and you will immediately interest these people.

Some points to consider

To create rapport with and to persuade socialisers you should:

◆ Show how you can support their dreams.
◆ Create a stimulating environment.
◆ Identify lots of alternatives.

- Be relaxed, enthusiastic and entertaining.
- Let them have the focus of attention.
- Keep things moving along.
- Do the unexpected.
- Stay with the big picture.
- Make the links to fun and enjoying life more.

Socialisers, when they present, can come across as superficial and lacking real depth. Their natural enthusiasm and use of superlatives can generate resistance, especially with analyticals. Socialisers sometimes talk themselves out of a sale.

DEVELOPING FLEXIBILITY

Perhaps there is no such thing as resistant people, only inflexible communicators. Perhaps resistance is a reaction to something you say or do and, if you did something different, that resistance would be replaced with acceptance:

By using our services you will become leaders in your field and beat the opposition.

This statement will appeal more to go-getters than carers. Sell to carers with go-getter values and you are likely to create resistance. You will be fishing with chicken vindaloo!

A useful question to ask is:

What do I need to say so the audience will want this solution?

SUMMARY

◆ Data and logic don't always persuade.

◆ Create the need if you don't want to appear pushy.

◆ Talk about what people will lose if they don't buy.

◆ You will create resistance by fishing with chicken vindaloo.

◆ Vary your influencing style to match the different audiences.

11

How the Pros Handle the Unexpected

In this chapter:

◆ being spontaneous
◆ overcoming obstacles.
◆ what to say when the unexpected happens.

Murphy's Law states that what can go wrong will go wrong. A train will only leave on time if you arrive late at the station. Computers never crash just after you have saved your work. If they do have it in your size, it is the wrong colour.

Presenters know that Murphy was an optimist! It is less a question of 'will it happen' but more of 'when it will happen'. What do you do when the fire alarm goes off, people arrive late or you drop something?

The inexperienced speaker gets upset and flustered. The professional integrates the unexpected into the presentation, even welcoming such moments as the source of humour.

BE PREPARED TO APPEAR SPONTANEOUS

The professional has 'outs' for these unexpected moments. All those witty ad-libs that professional entertainers have used for years are well rehearsed lines. The following is a collection of lines and gags that have been built up over the years. On paper they may seem glib or they may not suit your personality. Find the line that works for you, deliver it well and you will appear quick-witted, spontaneous and professional.

It is difficult to trace the source of these lines as many have been passed down the generations of entertainers and professional speakers. Why not add to this list and start your own collection of life-lines?

While the following lines provide the wit, you must provide the personality and deliver them with perfect timing.

MAKING SURE THE SHOW GOES ON

Side talk or uninvited comments

Had I known I was doing a double act, I'd have asked for more money.

It's OK, I can do the presentation on my own.

You haven't got a talking part.

I work alone.

He'd make a wonderful stranger.

Your mind goes blank

My mind is wandering and my tongue is following it.

I just wanted to pause a moment here in case any of you have lost your place.

You sweat

I'm leaking.

People arrive late

You're early, I'm still on!

Everyone in the room has just sang a song. Now it is your turn.

Good, we thought you'd never get here.

Have you got a note – a fiver will do?

People leave early

It's no use trying to get away, we've locked the doors.

Don't go away, it gets better.

Microphone feedback

Whoever you are, you can't land here.

Now that I have your attention.

You trip over words

I paid a thousand pounds for laser eye treatment and now my mouth gives up.

Lack of applause

That so amazes people they forget to applaud.

Ah . . . spellbound.

Now that the applause has died down . . .

When one or two people applaud

Thank you for the applause. Who was it?

Thank you . . . both of you.

No no don't . . . don't stop.

Late laughs

Come along, come along . . . I've a lot to get through.

No laughs

So this is where good gags come when they die.

Alright, let's spend a quiet evening together.

Extra loud laugh

Thank you, mother.

Just throw £10 notes.

You drop something

This is my first drop today.

This is what they call a floor slow.

It's an acquired skill.

They say the odd drop is good for you.

That's extra, that wasn't supposed to happen.

Something goes wrong

Some day I'll laugh at this, so why wait?

My philosophy is to live one day at a time and skip ones like today.

You are photographed

Hello, mother (as you smile and wave at the camera).

Try to make me look like Mel Gibson, will you?

Camera flash

That storm is getting closer.

Pager or phone goes off

My audiences always try that one! You're not getting out of here that easy.

Tell them I have already left, thanks.

The fire alarm goes off

Someone just tried to escape.

Coffee time.

Is this candid camera?

Mechanical problems

I love the computer, it multiplies the number of mistakes I can make per second.

Some . . . (the faulty equipment) are better than others. This is one of the others.

Visuals

Slide upside down: *I've changed my view on this point.*

Bulb blows: *Well now you are in the dark along with me.*

You trip or fall

I will now take questions from the floor.

> **The real pros excel not only when things go right but also when things go wrong.**

12

Go for it

YOU ARE REMARKABLE

By the time you reached your first birthday you had learnt to walk. This is a complicated neurological process. Despite the countless falls and bumps, you probably never felt a failure. By the time you were two years old, you had begun to communicate with words – a skill you learned without grammar books or language classes. By your fifth birthday you learned about 90% of all the words you use regularly in your lifetime. You are remarkable and you have a remarkable capacity to develop skills.

THE LEARNING CURVE

When we learn new skills (a language, tennis, golf or public speaking), we seldom progress at a steady rate. It is usually a jerky journey. One day you make great progress and then you slip back. There can be periods of stagnation, even hopelessness: 'I'll never manage this.' Remember learning to drive that car: 'Three pedals but I've only got two legs.' Today the complicated process of driving probably comes easy to you – you drive without having to think. The self-doubt and frustration you felt with your first driving lessons have been replaced with confidence and self-assurance. If you persevere with the skills presented in this book you, too, will be a confident, self-assured speaker.

FAILURE IS OFTEN THE ROAD TO SUCCESS

Successful people fail a lot. That's how they got to be successful, by learning from their mistakes. Each little failure on your road to presenting powerfully is just another piece of information leading you to success. Rather than take a fumble as a sign that reads 'I'm no good' or 'I'll never succeed', see it as feedback on how to get the presentation right. Now you can learn from the experience, change your technique and, in this way, you will succeed.

Find opportunities to present even if you are moving out of your comfort zone. As Emerson said: 'Do the thing you fear and the death of fear is certain.' Soon self-doubt and anxiety will be a distant memory:

> If you think you are beaten, you are.
> If you think you dare not, you don't.
> If you'd like to win, but think you can't
> It's almost a cinch you won't.
> Life's battles don't always go
> To the stronger or faster man.
> But soon or late the man who wins
> Is the one who thinks he can.
> *(Anon)*

Of course you can. Good luck!

Appendix 1

Pointers to Presenting Powerfully

WAYS TO DESTROY A PRESENTATION

1. Be unprepared.
2. Relate to your material more than your audience.
3. Apologise for yourself.
4. Repeat yourself.
5. Overload with information.
6. Tell a bawdy joke.
7. Have little variety.
8. Read your presentation.
9. Ignore time constraints.
10. Use slang or speak technical jargon.
11. Learn how the equipment works in front of the audience.
12. Make yourself so important the audience feels inadequate.
13. Direct your presentation at one or two people.

HOW TO GET YOUR AUDIENCE WANTING MORE

1. Believe in your message.
2. Believe in yourself.
3. Open with impact.
4. Close on a positive note.
5. Let your personality shine through.
6. Flex to the style of your audience.
7. Answer the question your audience will be asking: 'What's in this for me?'

8. Involve your audience and arouse their curiosity.
9. Use picture language.
10. Add variety and be creative.
11. Have an unusual slant or angle to your topic.
12. Spend as much time thinking about delivery and performance as you do about content.
13. Keep the focus on what you want rather than on what you don't want.

Appendix 2

Planning your Presentation

The following is a template to help you with the planning of future presentations.

Title

Date

Location

1. Objective
What I want my audience

To think To feel To do

Take-home message

2. Audience
Number of people – experience – background

What do they expect?

How will they benefit from listening to me?

Who are the key players?

Implications

Likely questions

3. Message
Brainstorm or mind map to generate ideas:

- Select key ideas.
- Develop subpoints.
- Decide on visual aids.

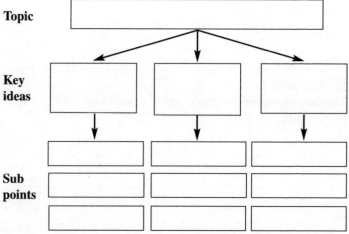

Remember:

◆ Add variety.
◆ Use picture language.
◆ Involve your audience.
◆ Use hooks and headlines.

4. Opening

Grab the attention of your audience and give an overview.

Suggestions:

```
Story
Startling statistic
Surprise
Shock!
```

Mention the benefits the audience will gain by listening to you.

5. Closing

Summarise the main points.
Answer the question: 'Now what?'
Suggestions:

```
Challenge
Call to action
Uplifting phrase
Take-home message
```

Appendix 3

Rehearsing

Rehearsing is a key part of preparing for a successful presentation. It allows you to become familiar with your material and to smooth the rough edges in your delivery. Rehearsing is an excellent way to develop your confidence.

The inexperienced presenter may want to begin by speaking to an empty room. After your first run-through you will probably think of new ideas and new ways to do things.

When practising, always stand and look around the room as if you were making eye contact with your audience. It is best if you video record yourself from the outset to discover how you look from the audience's angle.

The next stage in rehearsing is to have a live audience. Invite some colleagues or friends and give them some background to your talk. Explain who the audience is and its expectations. Ask them for honest feedback and go through the feedback sheet (see Appendix 4) with them so they know what to look for. You may even wish your 'audience' to ask questions.

When you receive feedback beware of responding with any 'yes, buts'. If you justify or get defensive, people will feel less inclined to be honest with you. You may invite the audience to give you some positive feedback before telling you how the presentation could be improved.

The final rehearsal takes place in the room in which you are actually presenting. Make this rehearsal as realistic as possible. Dress in the clothes you will be wearing, and use the notes, props and equipment as you will be using them on the day.

Appendix 4

Feedback

As a member of my audience, please answer the following questions about my presentation. Be as specific as you can about what I should do differently next time (scoring: 5 = high).

Did I get your attention at the very beginning? | 1 2 3 4 5 |

Do you think I related my talk to your interests and needs (did you benefit from listening to me)? | 1 2 3 4 5 |
What were my key points?

1_____

2_____

3_____

Do you think I made the transitions from one key idea to another smoothly? | 1 2 3 4 5 |

Was my take-home message clear, friendly and memorable?
| 1 2 3 4 5 |

Did I use language that elicited pictures in your imagination?
| 1 2 3 4 5 |

Did you feel involved? | 1 2 3 4 5 |

Was there variety in my presentation? | 1 2 3 4 5 |

Please score my style of delivery:

Eye contact	1 2 3 4 5	Voice	1 2 3 4 5
Gestures	1 2 3 4 5	Enthusiasm	1 2 3 4 5
Posture	1 2 3 4 5	Dress	1 2 3 4 5
Body movements	1 2 3 4 5	Credibility	1 2 3 4 5

What should I do differently next time?

_____

_____

_____

Appendix 5

A Checklist for the day of Presentation

Use this checklist to ensure your preparation on the day is complete and nothing is overlooked. This will give you peace of mind and help your confidence.

The room

Seating

Ensure everyone will have a clear view ❑

Arrange chairs to meet with your requirements ❑

Your position

Ensure you can be seen and heard clearly ❑

Position desk/podium as you wish ❑

Lighting

Use blackouts if the sun is shining on the screen ❑

Find out where light switches are ❑

Adjust lighting to your requirements ❑

Temperature/noise/ventilation

Adjust temperature control ❑

Open/close windows as required by delegates ❑

The equipment

Ensure audio-visual media will be clearly visible ❑

Test equipment ❑

Position flipchart so all can see ❏

Ensure there is plenty of paper and pens ❏

Bring spares ❏

Your material

Lay out your note cards ❏

Ensure they are in the correct order ❏

Place a pad and pen handy to make a note of
   questions etc. ❏

Keep handouts close by for distribution ❏

Ensure you can reach everything easily ❏

Your appearance

Check hair, zips, tights, buttons, tie, shoes, skirt,
   pocket flaps, etc. ❏

Empty your pockets

Bring what you might need for your personal
comfort – hanky for running nose, water for
dry throat, etc. ❏

Appendix 6

More Suggestions for Reducing Anxiety

Models of excellence

◆ Learn from people who present in a relaxed way.
◆ Imagine yourself as that person.
◆ Notice what it is like to be that confident.

Mental rehearsal – the 'warm-up'

◆ Picture yourself presenting as you want.
◆ Visualise in detail this sequence.
◆ Visualise handling difficulties successfully.
◆ Imagine the audience to be supportive.

Perspective

◆ You probably know more about this topic than anyone in the audience.
◆ Your nervousness is internal and will probably go unnoticed unless you draw attention to it.
◆ Ask yourself: 'Will it matter in five years' time?' Remember, today's headlines will be tomorrow's fish and chip papers.

Self-belief

◆ Believe in yourself and what you are saying.
◆ Look your best and dress for confidence.

◆ Recall a successful presentation.

Positive self-talk

◆ Replace negative self-talk with an image of what you want.
◆ Remember you are more than what you think you are.

Move around

◆ During your presentation move around in a controlled way.
◆ Gesture and point.

Memorise

◆ The first few lines of your presentation.
◆ Early in your presentation tell a story you are familiar with. Its familiarity will help to put you at ease.

Appendix 7

Developing Confidence

ANCHORS

The following is a technique from the world of neuro-linguistic programming (NLP), which enables you to anchor feelings of confidence and fire these feelings at will.

Think back to a time you felt confident. Go back in your mind to that moment and recall what you were seeing, what you were hearing and what you were feeling. Make the images, sounds and feelings of this memory more and more vivid so you recreate the feelings of confidence in your body *now*. You can anchor this feeling by bringing your forefinger and thumb gently together at the peak of the feelings.

The experience can be heightened by repetition (i.e. repeat the same memory or different moment when you felt relaxed, in control and confident). When the feelings of confidence are strong, anchor these with the forefinger and thumb. In this way you will stack and grow the feelings of confidence, which can then be triggered at a time of need by firing the anchor (i.e. bring the thumb and forefinger together).

MODELS OF EXCELLENCE

Identify someone you admire as a presenter – someone who displays lots of confidence . . . a real star. Pretend you are this person: walk as if you were this person, gesture as he or she would gesture, and so on.

You could imagine you are a director of a film based on your ideal life and you have cast the actor you would ideally like to play you. Direct your role model so that he or she makes a brilliant presentation (don't worry – your role model is used to constant rewrites and any number of takes!).

When you have it in your mind the way you want it, imagine it is now you in the scene, doing and saying the things in the way your 'star' did.

Rehearse the scene until you are completely happy with it.

CALMING

Before going on, close your eyes take at least ten deep breaths. Breathe in for a count of ten and slowly release. Repeat this and concentrate only on getting your breath into a nice, slow rhythm.

Here is something else you might want to try. Clench both fists really tight for a few seconds and then release. Screw up your face muscles tightly and release. Repeat this five times before you present.

About the Author

Shay McConnon spent 15 years in special education, teaching young people who had emotional and behavioural difficulties. He developed programmes to enhance the self-worth of these students and to improve their social skills.

These programmes were written up and are now a series of twelve titles ranging from *Conflict Resolution* to *Self-Esteem*. They continue to form the basis for many personal and social education programmes across the English-speaking world.

In 1988 he established People First, a management training and consultancy group that specialises in creating winning relationships in the workplace. People First is best known for its highly acclaimed Winning Relationships in the Workplace™ programme. This uses the latest in organisational psychology and leadership theory to create openness, trust and collaboration in working relationships.

The programme is being used by leading companies in Europe and the USA. The workshops are fully supported by a range of products, including workbooks, profiles, posters, memory cards and games.

Shay is a founder member of the Professional Speakers

Association and he speaks regularly at conferences on people issues. He consistenly receives rave reviews as a keynote speaker and has recently been awarded the FPSA. His flair for entertaining – he uses magic to illustrate key messages – combined with his academic background create a unique and memorable style.

For further information on People First and its range of products and workshops contact:

Tel: (+44) 1425 612610
www.PeopleFirst-Intl.com

Index